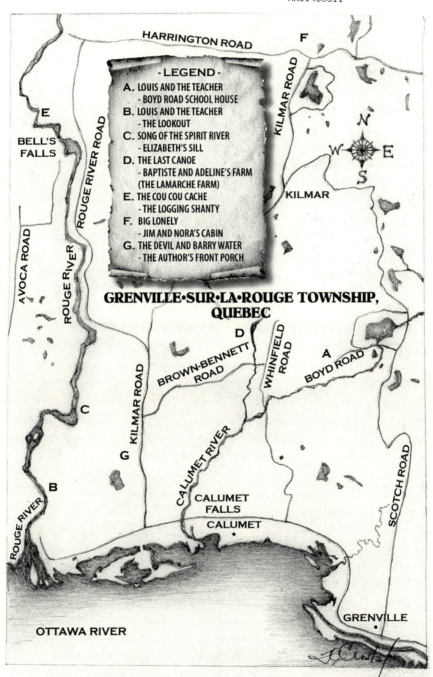

HARRINGTON ROAD

F

KILMAR ROAD

E

BELL'S
FALLS

ROUGE RIVER ROAD

ROUGE RIVER

AVOCA ROAD

- LEGEND -

A. LOUIS AND THE TEACHER
   - BOYD ROAD SCHOOL HOUSE
B. LOUIS AND THE TEACHER
   - THE LOOKOUT
C. SONG OF THE SPIRIT RIVER
   - ELIZABETH'S SILL
D. THE LAST CANOE
   - BAPTISTE AND ADELINE'S FARM
   (THE LAMARCHE FARM)
E. THE COU COU CACHE
   - THE LOGGING SHANTY
F. BIG LONELY
   - JIM AND NORA'S CABIN
G. THE DEVIL AND BARRY WATER
   - THE AUTHOR'S FRONT PORCH

N
W E
S

KILMAR

GRENVILLE·SUR·LA·ROUGE TOWNSHIP, QUEBEC

D

BROWN-BENNETT
ROAD

WHINFIELD
ROAD

A

BOYD ROAD

C

KILMAR ROAD

G

CALUMET RIVER

SCOTCH ROAD

B

ROUGE RIVER

CALUMET
FALLS

CALUMET

GRENVILLE

OTTAWA RIVER

Song
OF THE
Spirit River

By Gordon Fraser

Song of the Spirit River.

Published September 2016.

Cover photo: Mads Modeweg
Illustrations: Copyright © Jill Crosby.

Short stories.
ISBN 978-0-9952085-0-6 (paperback)
          I. Title.

PS8611.R3813S66 2016   C813'.6   C2016-904013-5

Printed by Lulu.com

Dedicated to
the wonderful people
and beautiful spaces
of Grenville-sur-la-Rouge
and Harrington.

Table of Contents

List of Illustrations

Introduction

"Find tongues in trees and books in open brooks," said Shakespeare.

There are many tales in the regions where these stories take place.

This is an old part of the country. Trying to find its beginnings is like pulling on a thread which has no end.

These stories come from brooks and trees and old souls; from those who walked before and left the legacies which live on to today.

I attempt to use names with respect, for without these names there would be no stories to tell.

Thanks to them for sharing their lives.

Louis and the Teacher

Louis MacCaskill was twelve years old when his father went away for the last time. His dad had been going to work in the shanties and harvesting for as long as he could remember, but this going away was different.

His father, Duncan MacCaskill, had come back from a trip to Grenville all excited. There was a war starting and soldiers were wanted. Word was it was just going to be a short affair; something to do with fighting the Germans and punishing the Hun.

Duncan told his son how he had fought the Boers when he was just a lad and here was a chance for quick trip and a little bit of pay. He should be back before Christmas. Duncan MacCaskill never did return.

Louis's mother had died when he was just ten. Their family owned little as could be counted as wealth. Duncan MacCaskill worked and tried hard, but bad luck had ridden along with him throughout his life. All the land grants from Grenville to beyond Harrington Township had long since been given out, and Duncan had no funds to buy; so he rented a log cabin off the Cedar Road beside Lake McGillivray.

That was where Louis grew up, living much of the time alone with his mother while his father went to whatever work might be had. When his mother died, he became the keeper of the house at ten; taking care of the cabin and the chickens and pigs, sometimes for weeks while Duncan laboured.

But the last time his father left, early summer 1914, he did not return. At the age of 12, Louis had to take care of himself. When the snow set in and he had not the hay or bedding for the two cows and young horse his father had left him, he went to a neighbour and traded board for the animals in change for splitting firewood. That way he kept himself and the stock alive over the first lonely winter.

He had gone to school when his mother was alive, and sometimes when his father was in the house, but now all school lessons stopped and he became a man.

Louis MacCaskill grew in stature and respect among the local community. By the time he turned 16, he was tall and strongly-built with black hair and dark, level eyes. He listened more than talked and when he gave his word a task would be done, it was. From his first job of splitting wood he went on to all forms of labour than might be needed from an honest hardworking lad. From ploughing to pulling weeds in crop fields, to running errands for the lumbermen and cutting and storing ice; Louis did it and did it well.

When coyotes scattered young stock, Louis was the hunter of choice. He knew every nook and cranny of the mountains and could locate a young heifer after she gave birth in the fields and get her home; his soft manner almost always avoiding a scrap.

The summer of 1918, Louis was 16 years, nine months old and he was nearly certain that his father would never return. There had been not so much as a letter since Duncan MacCaskill left the cabin door more than four years past. Louis saw newspapers with descriptions of great fights but he could make little sense of the names of the places: France, Holland, Germany seemed so distant and he could not relate.

That summer was when he was asked to split shakes for a new school that was being built on the Boyd Road. Not really more than two miles from his cabin and an easy daily ride on his horse – the only thing he owned. When the foreman arrived the first morning just as the sun was coming over the horizon and found Louis waiting with all tools in hand, he decided to hire him full-time.

It was not a big structure they were building: 32 feet long by 24 feet wide. Stone foundation, plank floor, planed wood walls and ceiling. There were two windows on each opposing side and a door and two smaller windows on the front. The back wall was solid.

As with all projects, this was made up of a thousand details to be worked out one at a time and they all came together smoothly. Louis laboured with Mr. Morrison, the foreman, and his two steady men; Hubert Bruneau and Mike Crooks. Every day they kept moving forward so that by late June, Louis was on the roof hammering down the shakes he had split and piled.

When the carpenter arrived to install trim and make the benches and desks, Louis helped him with the bull work of planing and sanding. Early August, he was back outside with Hubert and Mike, nailing up clapboard, working in the summer sun.

Louis was up at the top of the front gable one afternoon, finishing some detail and preparing to hang the Boyd Road School sign at the peak, when he heard harness bells. A carriage pulled by two fine blacks turned onto the site and a primly-dressed man stepped out, then went to the other side and helped a young woman step lightly to the ground.

Mr. Morrison called out. "Hubert, Mike, Louis; come on over here."

As they dropped their tools and brushed themselves off, the gentleman wandered around inspecting the desks and the smoothness of the walls. "Boys, this is Mr. Clark, school superintendent. Mr. Clark, these are my men; Mike Crooks, Hubert Bruneau and young Louis MacCaskill."

There were handshakes all around and words of praise from Mr. Clark as those men walked around. Mr. Morrison pointed out the quality work he figured his gang had accomplished and gave credit to them. Mr. Clark agreed.

The young woman stood outside on the stoop, looking over the rough yard and along the road to both directions, slim and straight. As Mr. Clark came up from behind her, he spoke and she turned.

"Dorothy, I'd like you to meet the men who built your school. Mr. Malcolm Morrison, Hubert Bruneau, Mike Crooks, and Louis. Men, meet Miss Dorothy Roberts. She is the Teacher."

For Dorothy Anne Roberts, just about to turn 20 years old and born near Ste. Anne's just west of Montreal, this was her first teaching contract. She was well-educated and trained in teaching methods, and had read the contract carefully.

She graduated from school knowing that she wished for more than a husband and a permanent home; if only for a time. She held a wonder for knowledge and enjoyed going over ideas with her friends; sit and talk. Not gossip but opinion. Through her teen years she learned to play piano and sports and graduated high in her class.

When she had noticed the open contract for a teacher at a new school in the outback, she thought "yes," then "no," then "maybe," and went to enquire.

The officials looked at her and her qualifications then sent her home while they spoke to her teachers. They received assurances that Miss Roberts had indeed passed all requirements with honour and shown herself to be a young woman above repute.

After a lengthy interview to be certain she understood the terms of the contract, she was given a train ticket to Grenville and the name of Mr. Clark who would arrange transportation and her room and board.

Now here she stood in the doorway of a brand new school in an old district. Her's was the task of making a place of learning out of a building and as she shook hands with the men, her confidence increased. "If they could create this place, I can take it from here," she thought, and thanked them.

As she bowed slightly, taking Louis's hand and thanking him in turn, their eyes met and a slight ripple passed between. Dorothy had a flash from a novel she read recently; something about 'kindred spirits', but that slid right away as the business of organizing began.

Louis went on with his work but he also had a flash. As he went back up the ladder, for a moment he was six years old and his mother was there; telling him of school and how he must listen to and respect the Teacher. He had been very careful to follow instructions; but that was long ago. He had not taken a school lesson since the spring his father went away.

So with the building complete, Mr. Morrison, Hubert and Mike left for another job. Louis was invited to join the gang but he apologized and said he could not leave the settlement this year; too many tasks to be completed. The boss told him if he ever wanted work or a reference, let him know. He gave Louis a bonus and a handshake, and an open invitation. "If you ever, Louis. You come see me."

Louis had only been off the construction for a week or so when a neighbour said that Mr. Clark had been around asking if perhaps Louis would be available to clean snow at the new school. Get firewood ready and make sure the well did not freeze over; that kind of work. Just part-time. Yes or no, Mr. Clark would appreciate a response and Louis could speak with Miss Roberts for details.

The next day Louis stopped at the school he had helped build just as the students were leaving for the day. Dorothy saw him swing down from his horse and noticed the home-made saddle for she had never seen such before.

She handed him the written details of what he would be obliged to do and the pay involved. Louis read it carefully, taking note of how much wood might be needed, and the labour involved, and decided it worked for him. He signed his name then handed it back to the Teacher.

After a bit of explaining details and small talk, Dorothy walked with him to his horse. "You have a good hand with a pen, Mr. MacCaskill. Did you attend school up here?"

Louis looked at her for a moment before mounting then said. "I had to give up lessons when I was 12." He glanced around and then met eyes with Dorothy.

"I am ashamed to say, Teacher, that I have almost no schooling."

He was about to ride off when Dorothy called.

"Wait please, just one moment if you could, Mr. Mac-Caskill." Louis turned his horse around.

"If you do not mind me asking, how old are you?"

"I'll turn 17 in six weeks, Teacher." he responded, then rode off east to the lake.

Dorothy was boarding in the Brown household. Only about one mile west of her school, it was an easy walk. The early morning air and the trees changing colour inspired her. With the sun rising over the hills to the east and mist lifting off the fence rails and fields, she was filled with a passion to set the school on a proper path.

She could do it, she was certain. Already, the black-
boards were installed; a stack of textbooks had arrived,
along with slates, pencils and a dozen items needed for
her record keeping. Then Mr. Clark appeared in his buggy
one afternoon and hauled in a big wooden crate

As students watched, he unpacked a large painted
globe and set it on Dorothy's desk. Then he took from the
box several other parts which he carefully assembled and
added to the globe stand, gave the globe a gentle spin and
said. "Well, boys and girls. What do you think?"

Ingeniously designed and geared, the globe spun on
its axis while around the world moved both sun and moon
in their proper relative place and order. Mr. Clark was
very pleased to be able to present it and the children were
fascinated.

Dorothy thanked him for the wonderful learning tool,
but Mr. Clark said it was his pleasure. Just one slight
problem: it took up about a third of Dorothy's teacher's
desk. He would have to find another stand for it.

His mood bounced back when he said to Dorothy. "Ask
young Louis when you see him. I am certain that lad can
fix you something up." So the globe stayed where it sat,
while Mr. Clark turned to other subjects of school contract
organization.

On her own at the end of her working day, Dorothy
pondered on Mr. Clark. A highly-respected educated
businessman with many resources at hand, had so easily
and trustingly passed a task to Louis MacCaskill; not yet
seventeen. Plus: he seemed to do so with confidence as if
certain when a job needed doing, "Ask young Louis."

Dorothy held no place in her life for gossip. To her,
people were as they presented themselves unless proven
otherwise; under the light of her judgement. But honest

information exchanged from one who knows to one who does not, is not gossip. And Dorothy never passed any judgement on information she received. She simply stored those bits in her own mind like a coloured-pencil box still missing some shades. Mr. Clark's faith in Louis MacCaskill was the first shade off the sharp blacks and whites she already had. She picked up more as the weeks went on.

The Brown household where she lived was that of a prosperous farmer and to that farm came local folk from all around the mountains. Dorothy met many at dinner tables and in the yard. She listened as banter passed between men while they exchanged news, and in those words Louis' name was sometimes to be heard.

"Damn, but he's good at finding them young stock. Why, my new young heifer, she bolted down into that rough stuff and I'd thought her lost for good..."

"Heard Louis was looking after Mabel's chores for a week or two. She took a bad slip so Louis is helping out. Mabel's foot hasn't been right since..." These overheard shades were carefully stored and never shared.

Monday evening at the end of the school day, Louis arrived carrying a large three-legged stool. He had made the top round out of a single piece of thick smooth wood and when he set it in the corner and placed the globe on top, it fit perfectly. Plus, it was solid on its legs, no shake.

Dorothy was admiring its steadiness when Louis spoke.

"It's a milk stool, Teacher. Longer on the legs and a prettier top, but a milk stool. Figured it would fit nice in this corner and the three legs make it solid on the plank floor."

Dorothy watched Louis admire the globe and its mechanisms. It was a fine piece of work all around with the sun moving with the seasons and the moon patterns passing through their phases. The globe was embossed and painted to show countries and mountain ranges and all the seas and major lakes.

Without being obtrusive, Dorothy showed Louis the Time Line, from where time zones are calculated as well as the degrees of latitude and longitude.

"Feel free to study it whenever you wish, Louis. Is there anything on the globe I might be able to point out for you?"

Louis looked at Dorothy, then the globe, then back to Dorothy.

"My Pa went off in the spring of '14. Only said he was off to fight Germans, I think. Never saw him again.

"Maybe, Teacher, if you could point out Germany on the globe?"

Dorothy did, and she showed him Holland and Austria and France; and the mountain ranges there.

Louis headed back out towards his horse then stopped on the stoop. Dorothy came to stand in front of him. "I understand that you missed your years for school, Mr. MacCaskill. Louis. And I see that you know a great deal without having sat on a bench.

"But Louis . . . Mr. MacCaskill, if there is anything I can help you with in the form of learning, please let me know. Books to read, grammar, numbers; if I can help, please ask."

Louis held his eyes straight on with hers.

"Teacher, I can cipher well. I read well enough for newspapers and items like Mr. Clark's contract, but I am very poor at writing words on paper."

He smiled. "Don't think I fit in one of those desks anymore, Teacher. Guess my time for learning is probably gone."

Louis MacCaskill rode off towards the lake while Dorothy Ann Roberts went to her teacher's desk and hung on tight.

As autumn set in and the nights became chilly, Dorothy found that her schoolhouse woodstove was always well-warmed up with a supply of split wood stacked behind. She saw horse tracks in the frost but sometimes, a week or more would go by without their even crossing paths.

In late October, she arrived at the school one morning to find he was installing the double-pane windows, so after assigning some work to her students Dorothy went out to speak with Louis.

She started with just small talk and the weather then went right to her question.

"Is there something I can teach you while I am here? There is plenty of room in the school, and I am certain we can find a desk for you."

She smiled from her eyes and he nodded back to her. "Teacher, just yesterday I had need to write out a page and I am very poor at that. What I know, I learned on my own and I think I learned more errors than rights. I would like to write a proper document."

By noon all the double windows were on and puttied. Louis packed up his few tools and Dorothy came over to speak. "When you can, Louis, when you have time, and if you wish, come to this school. You can sit and follow; learn how to write better."

When Louis did show up right at bell time on a Monday morning, Dorothy was very enthused. The children, though one was only a year younger than Louis, took his presence very well.

In that day's lessons, Dorothy taught as she always did: giving the youngest rote work to start, then the middle grades lessons to write properly. There was only one child in school near the top and that was Jenny McCarty who was 15.

Next year, there would be more students, and more ordered grades. But this year, Dorothy Roberts had 12 students aged from six to 15; grades one to seven, she figured, with a couple of slots missing. She hoped Louis could gather a little bit from some of that.

Louis would arrive at the school very early now that winter was setting in hard. The building was always warm and the steps were cleaned long before Dorothy arrived, and she was early. When Louis would come to class, he was always there before the bell; never late. But he did not always come.

Christmas season arrived and with it, Mr. Clark to carry Dorothy down to Grenville and the trip to Ste. Anne's. There she had a good reunion and all were positive about her capabilities. She shopped for some items in the city and by the time New Year's came around, she found herself anxious to get back to the solitudes of her backwoods job.

Her schoolhouse was warm and dusted when she arrived the first morning of the New Year and Louis MacCaskill arrived well before bell time. He came to tell her that he would not be in her classroom again before the snow-melt, but not to worry; her stove would always be lit, water in and the steps cleared. He had work to do among the shanties, he said, just until the ice breaks.

So she went on with her job of making a uniform base on which to grade her students and keep all interested and enthused. There was also paperwork to be completed and reports to the board, and the mile walk twice a day.

It went smoothly for Dorothy for her students and

parents all liked her and her relationship with the Brown household was fine. She saw horse tracks in the snow at the school and the place lacked no care, but she did not see Louis.

Louis saw her from a distance now and then, but mostly he and his horse were on trails packing in the parts and pieces needed to make the logging camps work. Sometimes 30 miles to deliver a saw blade and some plug tobacco.

February passed and March blew over. As April was about halfway through, Louis MacCaskill came to the school at bell time and took a place. When Dorothy went to his desk he said, "I can be here now and then, if it is still alright. On through to planting season which is when the school stops anyway; right?"

Every day that Louis showed, Dorothy had a lesson made special for him. Some of the hands at the camps had helped Louis to read smoothly, for many of the men were lovers of poetry. Confidence made his writing better and by copying out paragraphs from books he learned how to form smooth sentences.

Louis had a very good grasp of basic mathematics, but had never seen geometry. He would have thought it beyond him until Dorothy showed him the combination of numbers which prove a square; such as used by a builder. Then she demonstrated how angles from 90 degrees down to 22 and one-half represented stair lines. Then how tread length is calculated depending on angle.

"Rise and run," she told him. "This is what makes a good walking set of stairs."

In late April, there was no more need for heat and Louis had removed the double panes. By mid-May, the students were finished all assignments and spent the last of the month learning some outdoor games and completing exams. Just wrapping up; waiting for that last bell.

Louis MacCaskill had learned a lot of items which filled in gaps between talents he already owned. He was getting ready for hay harvesting time which would be in a few weeks. Then there was berry- and weed-picking to be done. Chores galore; Louis MacCaskill had never known otherwise and probably would never ask for more.

As he watched Dorothy begin the closing-up of the school house, he recognized the efforts and the abilities she had used to get him to sit and learn from her. He knew he was much better off in his world now because of her.

The writing helped him form clearer thoughts when dealing with people. He pictured buildings in ideas of level and square and when he saw a fine staircase he now recognized the relation between rise and run.

He held a wishful thought that he could give his Teacher something in return but he had nothing a woman in a city could use; and she was leaving for the summer in three days. One more night here at the Brown's on the Boyd Road, then two nights at a boarding house in Grenville, before taking a coach to Cushing then steamer to the town of Ste. Anne's.

Louis was adjusting his saddle when Dorothy Roberts came to say her farewells. There was a bit of small talk which came around to Louis' horse and saddle.

"Do you ride at all, Teacher?" he asked. "Ever own a horse?"

She explained that her mother and father were both good riders and they had given her lessons until just before she came to teach here. She shook her head slightly.

"Father insisted I only ride side saddle. Mother never rode with any other than side saddle but I wished I could have used an English style.

"Father would have nothing to do with those, but he did show me that using a side saddle does not mean a slow boring ride. We raced our horses against each other and he took me on trails alongside the river. I enjoyed those trails.

"Before you leave, Louis, I have something for you, if you could wait a moment, please." She jogged back to the school and returned with a leather satchel then opened it for him to see.

"I would like to give you some books, Louis, if you would take them – just four. This one: Tale of Two Cities by Charles Dickens. And this is a selection of four Shakespeare plays. And Sam Clemens' Huckleberry Finn for when you might want to laugh."

Dorothy took the fourth book out and sort of fluffed it in her hands.

"I'm not sure why I am giving this one to you. Just a feeling I have, and it has some lines I enjoy: Anne of Green Gables by Lucy Maud Montgomery. Hope they give you some pleasure."

Louis carefully opened each volume and saw they were signed: From Dorothy Ann Roberts (Teacher) to Louis Mac-Caskill, June, 1919.

They parted at that school house with a light handshake and a smile. But Louis's heart was heavy for now more than ever he wished to give her something in return. As he turned up towards Mabel Trineer's place, an idea started to form.

Mabel had a side saddle. It had not been used in years but was in good shape; just need a soaping. And Walter Bennett on Bennett's Flats has a horse he would lend; a pretty paint horse, friendly and gentle as a lamb. He gave his horse a touch in the ribs to get it moving.

Two mornings later at about ten he was at the boarding house door. Dorothy stepped out and saw the paint with the polished side saddle standing by Louis' rugged black.

"Would you enjoy a ride Teacher? I can show you some trails."

The landlady watched them ride away down Grenville Main Street with nothing but a bit of envy.

Louis took her north and then up the Whinfield Mountain. High up, they took a swing to the right then came out at a crystal clear lake set in low hills. A log cabin sat there and at Louis's call the door opened and an old man stepped out.

"Henry. I'm here a little early this week. How you doing? And Henry, meet the Teacher.

"Teacher, meet Henry," leaving Dorothy to stare into blue diamond eyes.

"Good to see you lad, and welcome, Teacher. Not often I have visitors."

Henry eyed the two horses for a few moments. "I forked one much like that black for many a mile."

He turned to Louis.

"Sorry, lad, but I got no food ready for you and the Teacher."

"Henry," Louis said, "You tell the Teacher about Calamity Jane and I'll make us bacon and beans."

While Louis worked, Henry told of how he and Jane once had to leave Colorado in a hurry, long time back. "Light a shuck" as he called it. They rode together to Seattle and boarded a steamer to Dawson.

He chuckled about Louiseville, just across the tracks from Whitehorse, and how Calamity ran the house and he worked the faro games.

"Had to hit out of there in a hurry too, after a game went wrong and half the town burnt." Henry said. "Decided that's enough. Told myself, 'Henry, get out while you can', and come to live here. Colder than Colorado but no need to look over my shoulder."

Early afternoon they left Henry's cabin and went west. They skirted between the hills and rocks until they came to Calumet River. They let the horses rest and drink while Louis fashioned up two fishing lines. She caught one trout out of the ripples then Louis quickly caught two more.

Louis cleaned the fish and collected some watercress and cattail heads. Then they crossed the stream on horseback and turned to the north. At a fork in the trails they went west once more.

Louis was a bit concerned about how far he should go before they turned back. "Do you need to get back early Teacher? Things to be done before tomorrow?"

She looked him straight in the eyes and shook her head negative.

So they spent two hours waiting for a fox to call out her kits, then more time watching those play. They slipped back to the horses and rode for a couple of miles until Louis led the way upwards through a pine forest towards the southwest.

The sun was low in the west when they reached a place where the trees stopped and the mountain topped out in smooth red rock. Jim picketed the horses before they walked up and out onto a massive solid rock mountain top facing straight south; polished flat to where it sloped off quickly.

The Ottawa River looked like a blue ribbon stretching across the landscape far below. She could see the Two Mountains to the east and almost make out the cross high above Rigaud.

Louis ferried up his saddlebags and some dead wood then went back down to the horses. He made certain they had grass and water with nothing to get tangled in.

As he did that, Dorothy took a seat right near the edge and watched the colours deepen in the sky. While she sat there, an eagle floated past, lower than she, and she saw the wind ruffle the small feathers on the great bird's back. Then it just arched its wings and soared away.

Over a small fire they roasted the trout with flour from the cattail and ate that with watercress and fire baked potato then set a small pot on for mint tea. By the last rays of sunset, Louis made up two camp beds, well separated, on the smoothest places. Over pine needles he spread on each a saddle blanket and a canvas slicker. He placed his saddle bags as a pillow for Dorothy.

Just before he crawled under his slicker to lie, Louis asked Dorothy if the mosquitoes were a bother. If so, he could add a bit of smudge and keep the fire going.

They were around but not really a nuisance, so she declined the smoke and pulled her slicker a little closer to her chin.

"If you can ignore them, sometimes they go away." Louis said.

Those were the last words spoken that night. The Milky Way came alive and the constellations turned against pitch black space. Louis and Dorothy lay watching the night sky and in each emotions rose, thoughts flew, and fantasies formed, and these flickered across the rock like the night breezes.

When the sun cleared the horizon in the morning, Dorothy stared in amazement. She could see past Cornwall to the St. Lawrence River and far beyond that, to the Adirondack Mountains; more than one hundred miles away.

They rode back down through the pines right to the village of Calumet. At the hotel there, they spruced up and ate a hearty breakfast. Then a pleasant gallop along the road to Grenville and back to Dorothy's boarding house. It was just past ten and her coach to the steamer departed at one sharp.

The landlady saw Dorothy and the solid young man swing down from their horses. She watched with more than a pang of envy as Dorothy smoothed her hair and patted down her dress. Her eyes held no judgement when Dorothy handed Louis the reins and spoke her last farewell.

Other eyes across the street in the butcher's shop did hold judgement.

They saw smiles and misty looks and saw how the teacher paused at the door to see Louis ride away. They passed the word.

Louis rode slowly up to Walter Bennett's place to return the paint horse. Something had changed in him. As he topped the hill and started down into Bennett's Flats it was as if his life had moved up one full level and a door had closed behind.

He bought a farm that summer with money earned from years of chores. The next spring, he built his own house and barns, bought stock and planted crops. When that was finished, he asked Jenny McCarty if she would marry him and she said yes.

He read journals and went to the fairs to find the best breeding stock and seed. Along the way his opinions became highly valued. Much later in life, he went with a carpenter to help reckon a difficult set of stairs. After Louis had laid out the rises and the runs and was getting ready to leave, the carpenter asked a question.

"With all you know, Louis, how did you learn all that?"

Louis told him.

"I really only ever had one Teacher."

Dorothy's stay at her parents' home in Ste. Anne's grew cool quickly. Her father was aloof and her mother distant. One afternoon after she had been home about three weeks, her mother took her into the den and closed the door; then pulled a chair up to sit knee to knee with Dorothy.

"If there is anything I should know about, Dorothy, don't wait. Your father and I have been speaking. He has a cousin in Sherbrooke and if you need to leave for a while, that is where..." she droned on. Her father entered the room later and put his hand on her shoulder.

"I'm hoping you have done nothing we will have to be ashamed of, Dorothy Ann."

Dorothy saw no reason to mention that her periods were come and gone and as she walked out of that den she thought of Louis's advice.

"If you can ignore them, sometimes they go away."

Somewhere in the depths of that night, a thought formed in her mind: if she had been carnal with Louis, then the eagle was carnal with the wind; as was the trout with water. She slept peacefully after and had a dream where she saw Henry as a young cowboy forking his horse, riding fast, lighting a shuck across an open plain.

She put together her more valuable books and jewellery and sold them downtown. She turned everything she had in savings into cashier's cheques with a bit of cash. In the bottom of her steamer trunk, she put paper and pencils, a case of film and the camera her father gave her for graduation. She stuffed the rest of the space full of all her clothing and three days later, took a coach seat on a train to Calgary.

She got off the train at Brooks instead and from her hotel window the first morning there, she saw the rising sun reflect off the glaciers of the Rockies from over one hundred and twenty miles away.

The general store owner was more than happy to trade a chest full of Montreal fashion for two complete sets of good riding gear tailored for her, boots and slicker tossed in. The saddle maker showed her a real nice roper's saddle he made to handle the rough stuff. She took the advice of a cow puncher and bought a tall dun horse; prairie-bred and born to run. During her days in the town, or out on the ranches looking at horses, not one soul questioned her motives or her past.

She rode that dun horse. She took pictures and made notes of the beasts and wild places and faces and Indians she met while roaming from Idaho to Athabasca. From whistle stops or post offices, she mailed envelopes to New York, London and Montreal. Her articles and photographs were published in newspapers and journals with credits given to D. Roberts.

She did instruct again later in life, but as a lecturer to academics and to halls full of young people who admired her knowledge and independence. She was pressed by a journalist one evening after a presentation and rousing applause, about how she did it.

"Is there any one person you would give credit to, Miss Roberts? Any individual perhaps, who might have inspired you to all that you have accomplished?"

Dorothy though for only a moment before replying, "I believe I really only ever had one teacher."

She never gave a name.

Song of the Spirit River

The Rouge River in Argenteuil County in western Quebec is a wild little river. Today, it has become a popular spot where people play on white water with rafts, kayaks and canoes. Few of those who come to challenge the rapids and dance on the eddies pause to think about those who have gone before.

Native tribes from ancient times knew the Rouge as the Spirit River. Then for 160 years, from 1808 to 1968, log drives took place along this waterway from as far upstream as Mont Laurier.

During the days when men used the spring rush to deliver their hard-earned harvest to the Ottawa River and the sawmills of Calumet and Hawkesbury, the Rouge was not a toy, but a way of life. To its banks each winter, workers came from all over Ontario and Quebec to labour in the forests and live in the shanties.

Beginning at the point where the Rouge enters the Ottawa, the water moves slowly. By the time the logs arrived here after their long journey, the work of the shanty men was almost done. In these quiet pools, the logs were formed into rafts ready for delivery.

Following the Rouge upstream, the river runs faster. The banks are rocky and come close together as the stream tumbles down through the mountains. The river must drop over 100 feet and pass over a series of chutes known as the Seven Sisters on its last run to the Ottawa. Above the Seven Sisters, the Rouge again widens out and runs smoothly, except for smaller falls and rapids all the way up to a big waterfall known as Bell's Falls.

The mountains in this area are not tall but rough, with cuts and ridges that make travel difficult. So in the early days, only a few settlers lived in the valleys and highlands that surround the Rouge. One spot where a family did live was above the Seven Sisters on the east side of the river.

That place, known since logger days as Elizabeth's Sill, stands covered with spruce trees planted over 90 years ago. Magnificent trees tower above a forest floor thick with the needles and cones of decades. Not many know or care that buried under that litter lie the foundation stones of a house and barn. Even more obscure are the remains of wooden fences marked here and there by mounds where the refuse from fields was dumped.

It's a place where silence does not exist. The river takes a turn, tumbling over one single step carved from the mountain rock. This type of drop was called a "sill" by the logger men and from this sill arises a constant din. In wintertime, the river gurgles as it passes under or around the ice which forms there. During summer and fall, a pleasant sound of water splashing on rocks fills the air. But in the spring, the Rouge crashes and roars in its mad rush to the Ottawa.

The Moors: about 40 acres sloping gently from the river's edge to where rocks rise forming long finger valleys that cut far into the surrounding hills. Facing southwest, with the river to the front and the fast-rising mountains behind, it is a pleasant spot to be; except in the spring.

To this place in the early 1800's came a family: father, mother and young son. Happy to be out of Ireland, willing to face life in the backwoods, the Moores bought the land nicknamed the Moors by early loggers who had worked there.

Thomas Moore raised his first log cabin not far from the shore, planting potatoes, hemp and buckwheat in some open spaces where white oaks had once stood. Then he built a barn large enough to hold his meagre stock and what hay he could scavenge.

Margaret worked shoulder to shoulder with her husband in the toil of pulling stumps and cleaning land. Her days began at the first light of dawn and ended when she could push herself no more. She pounded and wove the hemp fibres and ground the buckwheat into flour. Potatoes were carefully stored in clean sand under the cabin floor.

Ezeriah, ten years old when he arrived, took to the woods like a fish to water. He, too, toiled at endless chores every day, but always he found some time to enter those cuts in the hills that led away from his home. He trapped rabbits in the thickets and pulled trout from the river. From the first time his father let him carry a musket while he wandered, the Moore house rarely went short of meat.

In the early years, the Moores improved their piece of land and found that where they lived was a natural gathering place. There were not many who travelled the backwoods, but of those who did, some found their way to the Moors. Roving bands of Algonquin stopped, beaching their canoes in front of Thomas' cabin. Men searching for minerals arrived, asking about rock formations. Then came the loggers.

Logging had consisted of only a few men running small drives when the Moores arrived. The war with the United States was finished and Napoleon long since conquered, so the need for the huge oak trees which grew in this area waned low. But sawmills in Calumet and Hawkesbury were developing an appetite and now the drives began in earnest.

The Moors, which had been only snow-covered meadows in past winters, became a landing spot: a place where logs were gathered to await the spring rush. The water runs slowly both above and below the sill, allowing ice to form thick along the shores. The cuts through which the spring run-off pours down to the Rouge formed the paths for the skid teams as they went farther and farther into the virgin forest.

The sixth year that the Moores occupied this spot by the river was the first year a log jam formed at the sill - that fateful step in the river bottom just in front of their house.

The warm spring sun melted the snow quickly. On both banks of the Rouge for miles above, men laboured, pulling the fruit of their winter's work out to the ice and the expected break-up. Then a warm heavy rain fell, washing all the wood down at the same time. One single log jammed in the rock sill and faster than could be imagined, the river filled with ice and logs, the level rising fast.

Within an hour the water rose higher than the banks - so fast that the Moores had only time to hurry themselves and their stock to high ground, then watch the flood eddying around their house and barn. By late afternoon all they could see were the roofs of buildings showing between logs and chunks of ice. As darkness set, something cracked. With one awful groan the jam gave way.

The Moore family spent that night huddled in the pouring rain surrounded by their cows, horse, and what pigs and chickens they had time to find, while in the pitch black, the noises receded. Morning light showed their moor littered with ice and debris and no trace of their house or barn.

The Moores were not destitute for long. From out of the hills behind the log drive followed the loggers. When they saw the destruction caused by the jam they all joined in and helped rebuild. More than 50 workers; axe men, sawyers, carpenters and cooks, all put their efforts to a task. Within two weeks, a new house and barn stood, above the level of the flood.

The Indians whom Margaret had welcomed to her door returned with garments of leather and baskets. Far-flung neighbours donated the necessities so that by planting time, their life was back together.

Elizabeth Moore came into the world that summer: Sixteen years younger than her brother, blond hair, blue eyes, and pretty as a button. Her arrival changed the Moore household almost as much as the log jam. What had been a rough and tumble household took on a more gentle appearance as Margaret fussed over her new baby girl.

Elizabeth's arrival prompted Thomas to work harder on the property, planting more crops and planning a new vocation: supplying the logging camps with fresh foods in winter.

For brother Ezeriah, a new baby sister changed his life hardly at all. He loved Elizabeth dearly, stopping to cuddle her or to make her laugh at shapes of shadows on the walls. But at 16, he was rarely in the house. Besides his chores and hunting, he worked with the loggers and was looking forward to his second winter in the shanties.

After that log jam, the river bosses took great care to keep it from happening again. To the Moors each spring thereafter would come a crew of the best men; handpicked from among the shanties to closely watch the descent of the logs over the sill, able to act quickly should another jam commence. They did this partly out of compassion for the Moores but mostly because of the damage caused to the wood from being tossed around so severely.

As the years went by, the annual meeting at the Moors became a matter of pride for the shanty men. When the snow began to melt and the spring sun shone strong, the bosses would call the names of those chosen to guide the logs over the sill and on to the cataracts of the Seven Sisters. To be part of the gathering at the Moors meant recognition as the best at your trade and was an honour highly held.

Twenty-two years after Thomas and Margaret built their first log cabin, the yearly log drive was a common event. The Moores had prospered, clearing and using all the flat land available for cash crops and pasture.

Ezeriah had departed to enlist for military service, his sense of adventure taking him to the city and the recruiting office.

Elizabeth was 16, getting ready to be 17, when the shanty men began to prepare for the drive that year. Her hair shone honey-blond, though not so light as when a child, her eyes a most wonderful shade of deep blue.

Her mother's joy and the apple of her father's eye, she was known far and wide among the men in the logging camps. Those chosen to run the logs over the sill would see her and then stories would spread about the flowering beauty of Elizabeth Moore. Young men looked upon their comrades with envy as bags were packed for the trip to the Moors. They, too, wished for even a glimpse of her face.

Throughout the camps, the rough men held her as a symbol of purity and good. All were aware of her arrival at womanhood but not even the slightest hint of suggestiveness was permitted. To have harmed her would have meant instant death or worse to the perpetrator. Elizabeth, the girl at the sill; a gift to behold and the image of everything they laboured for.

Elizabeth was a hard-working child, always helping her mother with the tasks of the house. Still, her greatest joy lay with the gardens. Vegetables thrived under her care, but flowers did even better, especially those in her own little flower patch. At a sheltered place just about in line with the sill in the river, high enough to be well out of the way of the spring flood waters, Elizabeth had made a little garden with all her favourite blooms.

She knew the routine of the spring drives and looked forward to the arrival of the loggers. She liked the colour and the dashing spirits of the men who came to direct the logs: the men were so strong, so confident, and so gentle with her.

One young man chosen this spring was Duncan MacLeod. Nineteen years old, four years of experience under his belt, his ability with an axe and his talent of running over logs caught the drive boss's eye. He would be going to the Moors.

Duncan stood six-foot-four, wide-shouldered and narrow at the hip. Black hair and a permanent smile that only got larger when things got tough, he had become a favourite of the hands.

Duncan arrived at the Moors, strolling out of the forest on a beautiful spring day. Elizabeth saw him coming from where she worked, cleaning her flower garden and from the first time he flashed his big grin at her, she was in love.

Duncan could not have guessed this at the time. He

saw the blond-haired girl kneeling among the crocuses
and felt so overcome that his smile almost forsake him. He
wished he had been able to say something, or even give a
wave, but the shock of actually seeing Elizabeth allowed
him only one shy grin before she turned away.

The dozen or so loggers who came to work at the Moors
lived in a large cabin built many years before for the pur-
pose. Mrs. Moore did the cooking and provided the food,
forming another reason why men wanted this assignment:
a woman's cooking.

Elizabeth helped her mother prepare and serve the
meals, so her path crossed with Duncan's several times
each day. She was taken by the way he could handle himself among the crew of older men, though they rarely spoke.

Duncan worked all day trying to think of something
clever and pleasant to say to her, if he had the chance, only
to get red in the cheeks and trip over his own feet when
their eyes so much as met. Yet somehow, they both knew
something was special.

Elizabeth smiled at all the men and some of the more
daring took her hand or passed small remarks. But others,
like Duncan, felt so shy as to hardly acknowledge her presence. Still, she was the darling of all.

One whose shyness prevented him from anything
more than noticing Elizabeth was Charles Labelle. A mid-
dle-aged man, he stayed a loner and alone. Somewhere
behind him lay a personal tragedy of which he spoke not a
word, though rumour said his family had perished in a raging flood on his home farm far up on the Saguenay. Since
then, he worked the forests, living quietly and drifting
deeper into himself.

As happens every spring along the Rouge, the combination of warm sun and rain quickly melted the snow. Everyone knew that the number of logs would be high, for the winter had been good and the saw mills waited hungrily. The workers at the Moors were ready for the rush they knew must surely come.

They passed their time during the day chopping channels in the river ice, helping nature clear the path to the Seven Sisters and the Ottawa. When the first of the logs began to appear, mixed with great chunks of ice, the men directed all to the channel and open water. The work was hard but spirits ran high, laughter sometimes drowning out the sounds of the sill.

More ice broke under the pressure of rising water and the flow of logs became thicker. Men laboured from before dawn till well after dark, pushing with pike poles and running over the spinning logs to remove any potential snags before a jam could occur. The river ran smoothly.

Elizabeth enjoyed watching the men as they danced on the slippery logs; calling directions to each other, teasing and cajoling. She would sit among her flowers, safe on the sunny little ledge, and admire Duncan as he darted this way and that, using the logs as stepping stones. Or marvel at the great hulking strength of Charles Labelle when he drove his pike pole into a stubborn log and pushed it into open water.

Then one afternoon when the sun shone warm, a single tree trunk, ripped from the river bank somewhere upstream caught a root right in the middle of the sill. Within minutes logs began to back up as more and more piled against the big snag.

Charles Labelle was the first to see the jam begin. With amazing lightness for his huge size, he ran over the fast-gathering timbers and began to chop the offending log right through the middle. Duncan MacLeod quickly joined Charles and soon wood chips the size of saucers filled the air as the axe men worked in harmony.

The foreman looked on with great concern. His practiced eye watched the upper end of the jam for any signs, knowing the dangers of movement there. Two of his best men were at it while the others waited, ready to direct the logs when the jam did begin to break.

Charles and Duncan swung their razor-edged axes, both aware that at any moment they would have to dash for their lives. Then, when they felt a small tremor of the log on which they stood, they both turned and ran across the tightly packed jam. The severed tree trunk gave way under the pressure of wood and water with a great "crack", sending a piece of broken root flying through the air. It stuck Charles on the back of the head just as he reached the shore. He fell, knocked unconscious.

Several men pulled him to safety but he had been hit hard and the wound was deep. For all his troubles and the efforts of he and Duncan, the whole jam moved just a short distance then stuck again tighter than before.

In the warm spring sunshine, the river should have been running smoothly. Instead it now simmered, jammed from shore to shore, backing up quickly upstream. Logs and ice struck the higher end of the mass, adding their weight to the pack.

The foreman knew he had a problem, for the way the logs were stuck required that axe men cut on both sides of the jam; work hazardous to the extreme. When the logs began to move, there might be little time for escape. He must call for volunteers, single men preferred, and Charles was down with a blow to the head.

When the request went out, Duncan MacLeod's hand

was the first one up. Next, a big black man named Beauregard Bix lifted his high. He also had no dependant family and loved the chance to flirt with danger. While Margaret Moore stitched Charles' head, Duncan and Beauregard took their places, one on either side of the river, right on the foremost edge of the jam. They worked in unison, cutting the key logs, preparing for the rush they knew must certainly happen.

Elizabeth sat in her favourite place where the flowers of spring were showing and watched the men, especially Duncan, as they laboured. As the day wore on, the foreman made a decision; they would not actually break the jam until the next morning. The men had worked hard since before sunrise and shadows were gathering deep at the Moors.

By first light, loggers gathered at the edge of the tight packed jam. The morning dawned clear with blue skies and a light frost. The whole pasture at the Moors as well as the river to the west bank showed a sea of bark. Logs were packed so tight the surface was as solid as a floor. The Moores' buildings and Elizabeth's small garden at the edge of the sill were virtually the only places remaining free of timber.

Men took positions along the edges, loosening logs there and watching for any movement. Duncan and Beauregard made their way towards their work places, right at the very front edge of the sleeping mass. Elizabeth scampered around the tight-packed logs to her watching spot in her garden.

Tensions grew as one by one, key logs were cut to within a hair's breadth of breaking, awaiting only one last swipe to sever and snap. Preparations seemed almost ready. All along the edges, men watched and waited. Soon, when the last cuts were made, everything would go with a swoop.

At the very upper edge of the jam, the foreman kept his practised eyes peeled. All of a sudden he saw something which made him turn pale; a massive wedge of ice completely submerged coming fast, straight under the log pack. He had time only to shout a warning when the flow disappeared beneath the logs.

Somewhere under the surface the incredible weight of the ice struck the solid tangle of wood. Something had to move and that movement was up. Huge timbers rose like lava from a volcano. Beauregard turned from his axe work and saw the tumbling logs coming to engulf him. He looked at the distance to shore and then jumped into the water, preferring the chance of drowning to being crushed.

Duncan's position lay closer to some rocks than Beauregard's. He took a great leap as the first logs shot past him and was well on his way to safety when he saw Elizabeth.

Her little garden, which had seemed so high and safe, now stood at the same level as the mass of wood that circled and churned as if in some giant washing machine. Everyone saw her predicament at the same time but only Duncan could help her. He turned.

Into a wall of twisting spinning timber he ran, and he almost got to her. But everybody watched in horror as one pole shot up, knocking him into the froth, and Duncan disappeared forever.

Now Elizabeth stood stranded on a small stone in the middle of an ocean of wood and ice. She called to the men who were frozen in their tracks, too far away to do any good. One man made an attempt to cross the logs but made only a few steps before he sank and had to be pulled to shore.

Song of the Spirit River

Disaster seemed certain for with each moment the breaking jam gained force, threatening at any instant to carry away both Elizabeth and her small refuge.

Then, as if from out of nowhere, Charles Labelle was running over the churning surface. Where footing seemed impossible he ran, still wearing the bandages on his head. He stumbled and sank but pulled himself up again and continued. When he reached Elizabeth, he picked her up like a rag doll under his arm and turned to the nearest safety.

By now the whole river surface as well as the open areas of the Moors was a raging torrent as the unearthly force of the breaking jam gained speed. Charles shot into the middle of this, carrying his precious load, making only a short distance before his feet were knocked out from under him. He went down hard, turning to take the fall himself, landing on a sharp log.

Again he raised himself, cradling Elizabeth in his arms, and a great cheer went up from the men on the shore. His shirt was soaked with blood but on he went, safety and solid rock just steps away. Charles ran where it seemed a man must surely sink. Logs beneath him groaned and twisted, shooting up out of the foam like mere toothpicks.

Strong arms waited to grab him as he approached the rocks, Elizabeth clutching tight to his neck. Then a log reared right in front of him and he fell backwards into the water. He held Elizabeth over his head trying to protect her from the tumbling timbers.

Safety lay ten feet away but it might as well have been ten miles, and seconds turned to hours while Charles struggled to raise himself. Somehow he gained his footing and in that moment he gave a mighty heave, throwing

Elizabeth to those who waited arms outstretched.

They caught her and instantly she was transported to safety and high ground, leaving only Charles Labelle in danger. Free of his load, Charles almost managed to grasp the end of a pike pole held out by his comrades, but a huge log crushed him hard and drove him out away from the rocks.

Elizabeth had time only to turn when she saw the man who saved her go under for the last time. The jam was moving at full force and no living thing had any chance in the middle of that. Charles Labelle managed only eye contact and a weak smile to Elizabeth before he was carried under.

Nothing on earth could have stopped the flow of logs and water. With the power of ten thousand horses charging at the same time and a terrible groan, the jam broke loose. For more than two hours, the river spewed ice and wood until finally by mid-afternoon, the water flowed within its banks and logs floated freely.

No sign of Beauregard, Duncan, or Charles was ever seen again. Little wonder either, for just to see the broken and mangled timbers when they finally floated out to the Ottawa was enough to cause pity. A human body could never have survived.

The Moors ceased being an inviting spot that day. To Elizabeth, the sound of water over rocks became an unbearable reminder of the wonderful souls who died in her rescue; her one true love lost before they even shared as much as an embrace. She took a job in Hawkesbury, then found her way to Montreal, never to be heard from again.

Thomas and Margaret lived out the remainder of their days at that sad bend in the river with the sounds of the sill in their ears. Margaret grew more and more silent until one morning she did not awaken. Thomas gave up on his animals and his pastures, relying on the loggers to eke out a meagre living.

Finally the logging companies blasted the rock from the middle of the sill, booming the logs farther downstream closer to the Seven Sisters.

But among the shanties, the stories lived on. Tales of a beautiful girl named Elizabeth who once lived at the sill, and the bravery of the men who faced the fury of a raging river to save her. It became known as Elizabeth's sill; that place just above the Sisters.

Brush grew around the Moores' buildings, but nobody lived there after the death of Thomas. Occasional hunters or travellers shared the space with squirrels and porcupines until the roof caved in. Then it remained completely abandoned.

The brush grew to trees until they, too, were cut and those which now exist planted. It remains a sad place. Any who come to camp or sit on the rocks often do not stay long. Melancholy replaces the expected tranquility.

Today, dark spruces tower over the old Moors, stray daffodils sprout from a forgotten garden. Nothing remains to tell of those who gave their lives for another. The place is now as deserted as when Thomas and Margaret first arrived.

Yet if you were to make your way up to the top of the Seven Sisters, past the beaches where the rafting companies come ashore, you might find the Moors. There in the never-silence is a song, a lament for true love, sung by the Spirits of those who died for it.

The Last Canoe

Baptiste Lamarche sat on an old dock on the edge of the small lake. It was late October 1927 and this was Baptiste's birthday; he turned 90 today.

Baptiste still lived in the cabin he built so many years back, on the farm he owned in Grenville Township – nestled into the mountains with rocky hills to the north and gently sloping fields in the other three directions. There were trees all around Baptiste's farm with a long laneway that led to the Brown-Bennett Road.

Where he sat was on a dock set to run out into that lake of about 20 acres. Not really a lake, it is a depression in the mountain rock which at some point long ago had been flooded by a beaver's dam at a bend in the Calumet River. The lake is spring-fed and touched the river by a narrow shallow channel. The beavers have long since disappeared but they left their handiwork behind.

So Baptiste sat on a chair made by hand in the late autumn sunshine on the edge of what he had always called "the lake" and looked around. He did not see as clearly as he used to, but he knew all the details of all the fields and hills and the lake.

Even if he could not see it from where he sat, Baptiste Lamarche knew every twist and turn and ripple in the Calumet River; from his farm down to where that stream tumbles over the mountain's edge in long cataracts before ending at the Ottawa River.

He and his wife of 69 years, Adeline, had lived on this farm almost their whole lives. They raised their three children in the cabin which Baptiste built, not far from the edge of the lake. A smile crossed his lips as he saw in this mind his children as youngsters running over the green space between the dock and their cabin .

Baptiste gazed over the meadows to the woods beyond, although what he saw, other eyes might not have seen. He lived alone now that Adeline was gone. She had left him two years past on a lovely spring day. Their old dog, Bijou, had followed her, and had gone away this spring. So now, Baptiste Lamarche was the last to sit by the lake.

Reality showed the old farm had seen no repair in a long time. What once were ploughed and planted fields were now growing weeds and brush, though all lay brown in the autumn sun. His cabin sagged a bit and the door needed a lift to close tight. But that was not what Baptiste saw as he sat there.

Truth was Baptiste Lamarche was seeing some things now which were not visible to other eyes. Since Adeline went away, he sometimes spoke as if to her and sometimes she answered.

Baptiste and Adeline had three children together. Their two girls moved away from the farm almost as soon as they had finished school. They both married and had children.

Chantal, their oldest, lived her life just outside Lachute. Her husband was a white-collar worker; he wore a suit and tie to an office and used to get itchy when he came to the farm. Both Chantal and George were gone now too and he rarely saw his two grandchildren. But they were adults now.

Henrietta, their second child, stayed around longer than Chantal. She also found a husband – a good man. Henrietta moved all the way to Rockport, Massachusetts with Howard St. George.

Baptiste and Adeline went to visit her twice and over the years Henrietta came north to the farm to visit her

mother and father quite often. Baptiste had not seen
her in a long time now, though letters arrived once and
awhile.

Marcel was their third child. He looked like Baptiste;
tall and big-boned, heavily muscled with black hair and
dark blue eyes. Marcel had taken an interest in farming.
After he finished school, Marcel stayed with Baptiste and
Adeline. He had persuaded Baptiste to buy his first mow-
ing machine, then a mill to sort seeds.

With Marcel's help, Baptiste opened some new land
and pushed the forests back a little more. Later, Marcel
married Isabelle Plouffe and lived in a rented house not
far down the road from Baptiste's laneway. They had
plans of building a new brick house on the farm one day.

Adeline and Baptiste used to sit and talk sometimes,
about how Marcel was a natural farmer. He genuinely
enjoyed the daily nonstop labour and the land and herds
showed his enthusiasm; Marcel should be the one to
inherit the farm. He and Isabelle made a fine couple and
even though they had no children they ran a lively household.

Baptiste adjusted his seat in the chair and floated in
times gone by.

He and Marcel had ideas of purchasing another farm
and he even thought of some beef cows for a while. But
then one white birch tree split at the wrong time and in
the wrong place and before Baptiste even saw what happened, Marcel was gone.

It all took place so quickly; one moment he and Marcel were felling a birch in the winter time for next year's
firewood. Then on an axe stroke and in the wink of an eye,
the tree split and kicked back and Marcel was dead.

Instead of a load of firewood, Baptiste Lamarche that

day brought the sleigh to the cabin carrying the body of his son. Strangely, there had been not a mark on Marcel. The doctor who saw the body he said the tree hit so hard in the centre of the chest that Marcel's heart stopped.

That, too, was long ago.

This day was one of those rare, warm late fall days, long after the leaves have fallen and turned brown. The low sun felt strong and no breeze moved the air or rippled the lake; the sky a light blue. The odd wasp buzzed around Baptiste as he sat and looked over the place he called home.

He was 90 now: an old man. He still had the strong frame and his arms were sinewy but the days of being able to run a farm were gone. When Adeline was here he had always seemed to know what to do, and how to get ready for winter.

This year was not the same. The only firewood left in his pile was that left over from last. He was almost out of flour and needed some more canned goods. He just had not bothered to ask young Jimmy Cowen to pick up supplies last time he came by. Joe Mallette had offered to do his wood earlier, but Baptiste had said to wait and see what the year would bring. It had brought him to here and today.

There were many good neighbours now near Baptiste Lamarche's farm. Not like when he first built the cabin. The Cowen and Mallette families were close; James McCarty lived just to the west. Francois Laframboise had a fine farm to the north and of those, some stopped regularly to make sure Baptiste was alright. He was, and today he felt no need for company. He was content to sit here by the lake in the warm sun and look around.

If someone had asked Baptiste, and he answered honestly, he was not alone. As he sat there, Baptiste saw his days going backwards. There was not much to look forward to. He knew in his bones that this was probably the last of the warmth for this year; the season was changing. But he had a lot to look back on. His children were playing somewhere, and Adeline was doing her things around the cabin.

He had first come to this place when he just a boy, 1855 if he remembered correctly. Back then, there were no neighbours and no roads like today. When Baptiste Lamarche bought his farm, everything around was covered in trees, except for the lake. Beavers lived there then along the edges and Baptiste let them be. The lake was deep and with enough flow that they did not foul the water. And Adeline loved them from the first time they slapped a tail at her.

Baptiste's eyes went to the browned-over fields. When he first came up the Calumet River in his canoe, he had pulled into the lake to catch some trout. That was a beautiful day also, but in the spring when the forests were green with the new leaves, and the air smelled like pine and cedar with the sun's heat.

Baptiste got up and stretched out the kinks. He stood six-foot-two; he had been taller back then. His hair still held some blackness though it was thin and missing on the top.

He had returned, after finding the farm that day, with an axe and a shovel and a body brimming with enthusiasm and strength.

All that he could see around him started with a single axe swipe. But had he laboured. He girdled giant trees so they died standing then felled them one into the other; piled brush under and started a fire. Baptiste remembered the fires he made, and how he worked to clear what was left and wrestle the stumps from the ground.

Never had he questioned that he could or would clean

the land. The ground was black and fertile and the mountains to the north gave shelter. He held boundless confidence then, for he had wanted to marry Adeline from the first time he saw her and he needed a place for them to live before he could ask for her hand.

For a moment, Baptiste's muscles held that old strength as he walked off the dock towards the cabin. In his mind he was felling ancient cedar trees, squaring them, then hoisting one on top of the other to make the structure. The windows he had hauled all the way up from Calumet, as with the nails and hinges and stove.

As he walked along the path to his cabin, Baptiste was aware that probably tomorrow the frost would set in hard. Something had to change, for he was not at all prepared for winter in the mountains.

Baptiste knew winter. Before he owned the farm he had passed winter nights dug into a snowdrift like a partridge. Lain by a campfire at forty below where one side of his body steamed while the other froze solid. Those days were long gone, too.

What tomorrow and the hard frosts and snowdrifts would bring this winter, Baptiste could not predict. But it was today with the warm sun and the blue sky and the lake. 'Let the troubles of the day be suffice', he had been instructed and it was good advice. Now was not the time to change.

A bit of a dizzy spell came over him and he bent over to put his hands on his knees and catch his balance. He felt Adeline's presence beside him helping him straighten up and patting his back.

"Thank you, Adeline, and isn't it a lovely day."

"Yes it is, Baptiste. One of the last, I think," Adeline answered back. Baptiste agreed and she stayed by him until the spell had disappeared.

Baptiste took another look around his farm then back towards the lake and his dock. He had built a lean-to there a long time before he built the wooden ramp out into the lake. It was made so that a roof covered a space of about 14 feet wide by ten on the slope. It had worked well all these years, keeping the snow and rains off whatever he stored under. For almost all its years by the lake, the roof had sheltered Baptiste Lamarche's birch bark canoe.

He had built that too, after spending a winter in a Seneca village. There he watched and worked with his friends while a canoe was made. The next winter he made this one and it was still here; under that roof.

He felt strong again and he thanked Adeline once more. He saw the three children chasing each other under the apple trees and all felt good.

Baptiste Lamarche walked over to the lean-to and looked at the canoe lying on a frame, bottom side up. He felt his 90 years as the wasps felt the late autumn sun. For moments they buzzed as if early June, only to sit lazily in a shadow a moment later.

Baptiste was in the sun now as he ran his hand over the smooth bark surface and remembered the tree from which he had stripped that bark. The canoe was not heavy, in relation to what Baptiste carried most of his life, so he used movements which seemed instinct and flipped the canoe onto the ground right side up.

Baptiste looked into the canoe as Adeline stood beside him. It was made with a frame of shaved and curved cedar ribbing held together with the tough sinew root threads of elm tree roots. Over that, the bark of one huge birch tree had been stretched, inside out, to cover from one end to the other. The edges were framed from cedar also, as were the seat frames which each had a seat knit with catgut.

Where the front ends of the bark came together were stout pieces of curved ironwood as a bow. The back was similar except that piece which covered the joint arched a bit lower than the front. All the points where the bark was stitched to the frame were patched over with pine pitch.

Over the years and all the rocks and portages the old canoe had crossed, damage had been done to the bark skin and these, too, were covered in pitch. It still looked the same as the last time it was stored away.

That was the fall after Marcel had died. Baptiste and Adeline had paddled the canoe across the lake and onto the Calumet River. They floated downstream that day, the canoe needing only a touch of a paddle here and there during that sad trip. To where the river widens out suddenly, then runs shallow, almost dead calm in a pool before dropping off, they had floated quietly; remembering Marcel and how he loved to stand right at the very edge of the waterfall and look out over the horizon to the south.

Even though the river drops more than 100 feet, there is little noise; the water touches rock only far below. A trail exists alongside the waterfall, leading up all that height, winding side to side from the level of the Ottawa River to the very top of the Calumet Mountain.

They took one of Marcel's most precious items of life, a delicately-made doeskin bag amulet with a few omens in it, to the highest place and threw it over the waterfall so the pouch fell into the falling river to be lost in the mists below.

Baptiste was remembering these things, and again as if moved by nature, he slid the canoe out onto the dock and let it slip into the water. It floated light as a leaf and laid there with no tether.

"Want to come for a ride?" Baptiste asked Adeline.

"A paddle around the lake before the ice sets in, wife? What do you think?"

"Not right now, Baptiste." Adeline replied.

"It is the perfect day to gather in the ginseng roots from over under the maples. Keep you strong, Baptiste." Adeline smiled and thought for a moment.

"You go, Baptiste. I'll walk over and gather the roots. By the time you have made a round, I should be done. When my work is finished, I can meet you on the other side, and you can give me a ride home. What do you think, Baptiste?"

The lake shimmered smooth as glass and probably tomorrow morning it would be iced over, and she agreed that it was a lovely afternoon for a ride.

"Ah, Adeline," Baptiste said. "You always know how to make things work out, don't you? I think I'll take the old canoe for one last time, and see you on the other side."

Baptiste stooped over and put one foot in the canoe and it stayed firm so he put the other in and bent to sit on the seat. He first sat the way he did when he was a young man, on the gut mesh with his feet pressed against the outer bottom ribs and his knees tight together.

The old joints did not like that position so he adjusted his legs straight out. That was good but today he felt the need of a back rest so he just slid till he rested on the bottom of the canoe, legs stretched out and his back against the seat.

Baptiste sat there for some moments then gathered up his maple-wood paddle. Adeline had carved this one for him as a Christmas gift and it was perfectly balanced. Its paddle end showed wear where it had bumped rocks and the shaft and grip were worn to fit his hand. It felt natural for Baptiste to dip it into the water and give a tug.

The old canoe sat light in the water but barely moved with Baptiste's effort. So Baptiste dipped once more and pulled harder. The water just off the dock had grown some weed and that held the canoe, but on Baptiste's third try, the canoe set to motion and glided slowly out into the lake.

Baptiste relaxed against the seat and felt the slow movement.

"You old canoe." Baptiste spoke to the canoe for he had done that a lot over all the time he had sat in that seat.

"You are slow today, my friend. I remember when you used to move through though lily pads like a pike in the shallows."

Baptiste gave another stroke of the paddle and the canoe moved a little quicker as it cleared free of the weeds.

"What's with you, canoe?" Baptiste asked. "Why you not want to go quick today? My old friend."

This day the canoe spoke back and it spoke in a voice that sort of reminded Baptiste of wind in the leaves of a poplar tree.

"Baptiste, my maker. You do not push like you once did. I remember how your arms could drive me up a rapids. There is no rush today, Baptiste. This is our last ride."

Baptiste took another stroke and the canoe moved faster a bit, out into the blue flat water. He looked over his workmanship from so many years ago.

"You still float well, canoe, and you look as you always did," Baptiste said and the canoe answered back in its whispering voice

"You built me such, Baptiste, to last and to do that for which I was created. As our creator made you."

Baptiste pondered this while he pulled lightly and the canoe moved on.

Song of the Spirit River

"Not quite our last ride, canoe. We still have to pick up Adeline on the other side."

The canoe did not respond.

They floated out to the centre of the lake and the slight current naturally took the craft slowly from there towards the channel which leads to the Calumet River. It was about dinner-time but Baptiste was not hungry and had no thought of a clock.

He ran his weathered and work-hardened hand over the smooth outer side of the birch bark canoe and the canoe spoke to him.

"Do you remember the day you cut me, Baptiste? I was a tree and had watched the seasons go by and knew nothing else until you saw me and I saw you." Baptiste did but he remained quiet.

"I died as a tree that day, Baptiste. But I was reborn. You took my skin and stretched it over ribs of cedar. You held all together with the root of the elm and gave me life with the blood of the pine. I died as a tree and was reborn as a canoe. I believe it is greater to be a canoe than a tree. I have seen both sides"

"I was born a man, canoe." Baptiste replied, and canoe agreed but said nothing.

They floated together as they had over endless miles of water and Baptiste remembered once when they crossed Lake Superior and for two days he saw no land, nothing but water. As they moved through the channel and into the smooth flowing Calumet River, Baptiste asked the canoe a question.

"Do you remember the great lake, canoe? How there was nothing but you and I and the long rough rollers? I was afraid sometimes but you got me across."

"It was your faith that got us across, Baptiste," Canoe

replied.

They drifted down the river.

Earlier in the year, the Calumet River would have been canopied with tree leaves and in mostly in shadow. It is a small river which flows strong in the spring and sometimes freezes almost solid in the winter. There are no rapids to speak of between Baptiste's farm and the top of the Calumet Mountain.

Certainly nothing to concern Baptiste and the old canoe.

"We can't go too far, canoe," Baptiste said. "We have to pick up Adeline. She will be done her chores soon. Don't want to keep her waiting, do we canoe?"

"I know where she waits, Baptiste. We still have a bit of time," canoe spoke with its wind voice. They floated.

The river was dappled with the shadows of bare branches blocking the mid afternoon sun; the river held enough water to float the light craft and cover the rocks in the slight ripples of Calumet River.

"Do you remember how we brought Adeline up the river for the first time, canoe?" Baptiste asked.

"She was as fair as you were strong, Baptiste. I remember well. Just after the big float of canoes down through the Long Sault and she was so lovely. I remember that day well." The canoe spoke and Baptiste just went with the memories.

"You had her in my bow seat, Baptiste, and I was proud to be a part of that joining of the canoes. There were many like me that day, and one great one, longer than four of I, with a great lady in the centre. But she paled compared to Adeline."

"Yes, canoe. She was lovely that day with her curly hair the colour of a robin's breast, and eyes that sparkled like sun on tiny waves. I was proud of you, Canoe. We sat together, you, me and Adeline at the bottom of this river below the falls and I asked her if she would marry me. It took more courage to speak those words than to paddle out onto that great lake, but when I did she said yes."

Baptiste pondered for a few moments and continued. "You are right, canoe. There were many like you back then. I believe you are the last of your kind."

Canoe agreed and they floated.

The birch bark canoe moved quicker for a bit. It slid down some slight rapids and slipped under the bridge at the Brown Bennett Road, then slowed as it went around a bend.

The wind whisper voice of the canoe spoke again.

"Remember how many times we went up and down this river, Baptiste, while Adeline made the home?"

"I do, canoe. I would leave you at the top of the falls and walk the trail down to Calumet to get what she needed to put it together. Then you would bring me back to her. How many times, canoe? How many times?

"Remember when Adeline made her brooms and spoons from ash wood. We took them, you and me, canoe, down this river. I would carry you and her brooms down the rocks beside the falls to the Ottawa."

"Yes, Baptiste. Then I would carry you across the river and to the town where people waited for her brooms." The voice fell silent and they floated.

The Calumet River flows only about twenty feet wide below the bridge at the Brown Bennett Road and without rapids, through forests and open fields. It takes twists and turns and flows straight for stretches. Over this water Baptiste floated, needing nothing more than to drag his paddle to stay within the banks.

While they floated on water, both canoe and man floated in consciousness; for one had been, and the other about to become. Baptiste's mind moved over his years like his canoe moved on the river.

He saw Adeline as a young woman, flashing blue eyes and flaming red hair, stuffing moss between the timbers of their cabin and for a moment she was turning and smiling at him; hands dusty with oakum as she took his face and kissed him.

Then she was baking the first loaf of bread in the stove he had laboured so hard to get up that trail by the falls.

The canoe floated into an open space as Baptiste remembered when their first child Chantal had been born, with no help but from him. How he and canoe had hurried along this river the first time he had to leave Adeline and Chantal alone at the farm.

But Adeline was so strong. She hardly slowed down and that summer, the three laughed in the canoe on the lake on a lovely sunny day.

When Henrietta was born, Mrs. Mallette was there to help with delivery. Baptiste had passed nervous hours outside the cabin while she stayed inside with Adeline. He spent that time spreading some pine pitch on a repair to the canoe, making a mess with his efforts.

Canoe remembered that day well.

The sun was getting lower in the sky now, still not a breath of wind – but a chill when they passed through shadows, moving slowly but certainly forward.

Marcel had been born in the cabin also, though for his birth Baptiste was not nearly so nervous. By then the farm was cleared to about 50 acres and he had a horse and cows and chickens and pigs. Marcel grew strong quickly and pretty well as soon as he could walk, he was pestering the rooster or out in the calf pen.

Song of the Spirit River

Canoe did not get used much by that time. Chantal and Henrietta floated in it on the lake when the water was calm and warm. Marcel played with it on the lake and now and then on the Calumet River. But mostly, it sat by the dock or under the lean-to; until it was hauled down for that ride to take Marcel's memories and toss them into the mists.

Canoe remembered that ride, too, as they went from sun to shadow. The wind spoke.

"Marcel was not sad that day. I cried with you and Adeline for your sorrows, Baptiste. Though you were so sad you heard me not.

"When you and Adeline pushed me back up this river that day, it was not the fall currents that made me heavy, it was our hearts."

They both remembered an early autumn afternoon when the leaves were in colour, though the world was black and white.

If anybody would have been watching, this late October afternoon, they would have seen an old man slouched in an ancient birch bark canoe floating along the Calumet River on the quiet steady stream.

He and the canoe were about a mile from where the little river widens into a quiet pond before passing through a gap in the rock. There it tumbles almost vertical in one splendid waterfall all the way down to the level of the Ottawa River from the top of the mountain behind Calumet.

No one was there to see and they floated.

They passed beneath the shade of some pines and a chill brought Baptiste's thoughts to the coming winter.

"Winter is almost here, canoe. Soon, you will go back to your shelter." Baptiste pondered for a moment.

"I don't know what I will do this winter, Canoe. My

woodshed is almost empty and I'm nearly out of beans."

Canoe remained silent while Baptiste considered.

"I am old, Canoe, and I think I cannot make another winter. What happens?"

Baptiste slouched lower in the craft as the weight of years came on him. He let the paddle slip out of his hands, although he was not aware of that.

They were passing through mixed sunlight and shadows, the sun losing its heat as it lowered in the sky; the water calm and steady. The wind voice of the canoe spoke again.

"My maker, I was a tree and for a time I believed I would always be a tree. Where I stood and watched the seasons pass was my world. I saw spring flowers bloom and winter snows fly, as have you.

"My seed spread, as has yours. I, too, was feeling the weakness of a body. My leaves were sparse, and small trees grew around.

"Then you appeared to me, my maker, and gave me new life and my worries turned to joy. It is greater to be a canoe than a tree. I could not have known such save for you."

They were both silent and there was no sound except for birdsong in some pine trees as they turned the last bend where the river widens out and loses its current. The sun was low in the southwest sky making the open flat water reflect its rays.

For Baptiste, the wind was whispering through poplar leaves and the words were clear.

"When we were on that great water, Baptiste, faith took us to the other side though for a time we saw not either shore; if not for faith we would surely have been lost.

"You loved me as I loved you all these years, Baptiste. And you love Adeline as you do your children and the farm;

and me. Love is what put strength in your body. Love is what made your children and me and all we have seen in our travels.

"Adeline's love for you is boundless, Baptiste, and now it is time to find her. We will ride home together."

Baptiste looked out over the pool as it reflected the setting sun's colours and for a moment it blinded him.

"Where is she, canoe? I cannot see."

"She waits for us, Baptiste, by the shore. She gets in now." The canoe bumped against some stones at the edge of the pool as the slight current carried it.

Adeline stepped lightly into the front and sat facing Baptiste so she blocked the strong sun and Baptiste could see her clearly now, outlined by the glowing sky.

"Husband," Adeline said.

"Right on time, and isn't it a lovely day for a canoe ride. Our last for this season, maybe."

Adeline smiled one of those lovely smiles which had inspired Baptiste since the first time he saw her so many seasons past.

She leaned forward and kissed him sweetly on the lips just as the canoe went over the edge to disappear in the mist below.

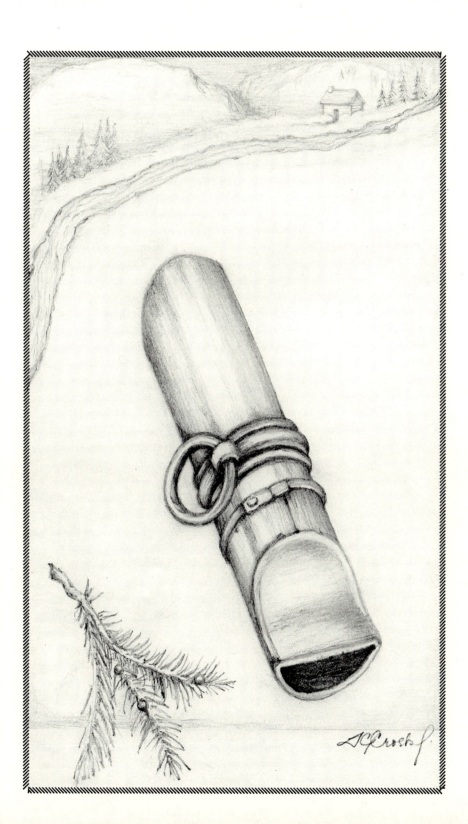

The CouCou Cache

It was late winter, 1858, when Constant Palache tromped into the yard of the logging shanty, just above La Belle's falls on the Rouge River. He walked up on snowshoes from Calumet on the edge of a storm; wind moaning through the tall trees and snow falling hard.

He was here to check on production and to plan for the spring break-up which, though weeks away still, was a task his uncle showed him was best planned well in advance. Never leave anything until the last moment, he had been taught, and he followed that lesson well.

So the shanty men were not surprised to see him appear out of heavy falling snow from the river trail as they finished their day's work. Constant Palache knew all the men in this camp, as he did throughout the far-flung shanties. And all the men knew of Constant Palache, for his reputation as a timber man was legendary. Stories told how he and Big Joe Montferrant had stood back to back against 19 men in a Renfrew tavern; of his time as a Voyageur with Jean Courteau, and more.

Constant Palache greeted each man he met as he made his rounds, snow drifting and darkness setting in. Everyone was finishing up for the day, making certain that the camp would be ready for the morrow and the digging out they knew was coming.

Inside the shanty the winter wind whistled around the chimney; the storm was growing stronger. Men came in out of the swirling snow with stamping of boots and slapping and shaking of coats. The stove in the centre of the room glowed red.

The cook, a crusty old hand and veteran of countless log drives, watched the faces of the shanty men as they entered the big lamp-lit cabin: Charbonneau, the thin wiry one who runs behind the skid team as the logs are snaked out from between the stumps. Bernard, the scaler and sharpener; and O'Riley, self-proclaimed champion with axe or fists. The cook knew their chores for the day were almost finished while his, the task of filling these bellies and keeping the bodies strong, had hardly begun.

More men entered. Plates were set along both sides of the plank table and soon dishes of steaming food beckoned as faces lined with sweat and fatigue turned to eye the feast. But they knew the rule that when the boss was on site, no one took his place until Constant Palache was in and seated.

Talk was small and moments seemed long before the door opened and the bulk of Constant Palache came in out of the dark and the storm. A glance around the room and a nod of his head showed all was in order. Everyone's task had been completed to his satisfaction and the meal would be served. A hard master but fair he was, and he kept the camps and the men working at their best.

What had been an orderly table was reduced to empty plates as the men ate in near silence. Grunts of appreciation and requests to pass platters were the only sounds until chairs were pushed away and pipes lit. Big pots of scalding hot tea took the place of dirty dishes as men stretched and yawned with the warmth and full stomachs.

The wind outside the shanty rose in a gust causing a whistle in the stove pipe and the cook dropped the pile of tin plates he was carrying to the wash basin. The men who stopped what they were doing to look caught a glimpse of the old man's face become white, though he turned so not to be seen.

Chancy, called such for the risks he takes while running logs through the spring rapids, was one who remarked on the cook's face and he called across the room. "Hey Cookie. Why you looking so pale? You see a ghost in the corner?"

Only a small ripple of laughter went up, for everyone knew you don't ridicule the one who makes the food. The cook was a good-natured soul and he could take a joke, but the comment went unheeded as wind howled through the winter forest.

The cook, forgotten for the moment as he picked up the mess, was not thinking about the teasing. There was something in the storm, and this night, which had him remembering a tale told to him long ago. He had to concentrate hard to do his job; his mind much on the sounds of the winds.

O'Riley, known to be afraid of no man, picked up the tail end of the remark.

"In the future, ghosts will disappear. By the time a new century arrives, no one will believe in haunts. Besides, who in their right mind would fear something you cannot see?"

Charbonneau got up from his chair and went to the stove. He stood there for some time, rubbing his hands together, enjoying the warmth. "Aye, you're right about times changing, O'Riley lad. But I think we shall always share this world with others we cannot see." He turned and asked over his shoulder "What say you, Constant Palache?"

Constant sat where he was making entries in a ledger, away from the main table at a desk near one of the cabin's two windows. The sound of his name being called took him from his thoughts and he looked at the teamster, asking him to repeat.

Charbonneau asked again. "Do you believe in things we cannot see? Foreman, Sir."

The winds outside the log structure moaned and for a moment the shanty shook slightly under the force of one strong blast. Constant Palache set aside his pencil and stared out the window, waiting for the storm to subside, using the time to think about what he would say.

"Aye my lads, I say like Charbonneau. They are all around us, those we cannot see. Never do I scoff at the spirits. But that was not always my way."

The cook, still forgotten as he stacked plates and hung cooking pots, was listening closely to the chatter of the men as ghosts and goblins were discussed.

O'Riley told about the wee ones who lived among the stones in the old country of Ireland, expressing disdain for those who believed in such. He laughed as he recounted his grandfather wasting good whiskey on those full-moon nights, when he would set a glass of his best inside the fairy rings.

Delhi, the huge black man whose strength was unmatched by any in the room, recounted how his mother took great caution not to offend the Voodoo doctors at her home in the Bayous far to the south. He spoke of spells and apparitions and dolls.

Around the shanty, man after man told his opinion of denial or belief until all had been heard; except the cook. Outside, the storm grew more intense and as the winter wind howled the men moved closer to the red-glowing stove. The cook remained in his corner though his work was complete.

Constant Palache, who had quit his numbers and ledgers, took a seat with his feet to the stove and lit his pipe. He was about to say something when a tremendous blast of wind blew the door open and for an instant everyone turned to see. By some trick of that awful gale, in that moment a small whirlwind, outlined by the heavy falling snow, circled the opening then entered and dissipated into a heap of white on the floor.

Faster than what might be imagined for an old body, the cook was across the room, slamming the door shut and jamming the bolt in place. All who had been looking at the doorway now found themselves staring at the ghost-white visage of the old man.

"What are you looking at?" The cook snarled. The gnarled face glared back at each of the men. For a moment, the silence in the shanty was complete.

It was as if something had entered the shanty with that snow devil and all were aware of the change. Delhi's squeeze box fell silent. The checker game between Chancy and O'Riley was forgotten. Bernard stopped whetting the axe he had been working on; he, too, frozen in his place.

The wind moaned sad. A shutter banged and all jumped. Constant Palache was the first to move, getting up to fasten the loose board. He stood there for a time, his attention held by something in the swirling darkness. Before leaving the window he paused to look out one more time, shaking his head slightly as he turned back towards the room and his seat.

The cook remained, back to the door, staring at the gawking faces. "You men who mock the spirits, what do you know? It's here. Listen. Don't you hear it calling?" The old man cocked his head to the sounds outside.

Constant Palache sat with his elbows on his knees.

Delhi's blackness was darkened more by the shadows cast by lamplight. O'Riley and Chancy remained face to face over the unfinished checkers game. Bernard held tight to the razor-edged axe.

The storm blew hard, moaning and crying through cracks in the shanty and the shingles overhead. But above these sounds were others, like voices calling over some great distance or time.

"You hear it, don't you?" The cook's cragged face was still turned, ear towards the door. "I knew it. When a storm blows like this in these forests the Windigo walks. There, it calls again! It is calling one of its own."

O'Riley, not to be intimidated by man nor ghost, tossed down the checker in his hand. He rose from his seat, opening his mouth to speak but the cook stopped him with an outstretched hand, palm first. "Listen," the old man said. "Listen to it speak."

It did not take imagination to hear voices filled with agony in the winds which howled over the roof and, although the stove was packed full, the room felt cold. The men huddled close to the glowing metal, no one thinking of his cot, preferring company to solitude.

Constant Palache sat with his head in his hands. The cook stared at him. Time seemed thick as molasses before the old man spoke.

"Is it you, Constant Palache? Is it you it has come for?"

Nothing more was said until Delhi jumped, tossing his squeeze box to the floor in his fright, white eyes huge in the dark face. "Something's out there Boss, something was looking in! There! Again!"

All eyes turned to the window; all except the cook and Constant Palache.

Constant raised himself, rubbing big hands over his

rough face, then stood and went to the cook. He took the old man to a chair and sat him down.

The storm now blew so hard that the cabin creaked and groaned under the pressure. Constant spoke. "The Windigo, Cook; you are right. It walks tonight, though perhaps it only comes to remind me of another place and another time.

"Forty years ago this night, my uncle Cyprien Palache disappeared in a storm like this and was never seen again. I remember it like it was yesterday; up at the Cou-Cou Cache."

The cook, calmer now, stared at the foreman. "Then the story is true, Constant. Tell us what happened."

Delhi, still wide-eyed from the vision at the window, grew even more so as he listened to the cook. The other men's attention was on Constant while he walked to the window and looked out. He stood there, seeing the stumps which surrounded the shanty, thinking of how they looked like tombstones as the snow drifted round.

Chancy broke the silence. "Tell us Boss."

Constant returned to his place by the stove. Delhi was seated again; his squeeze box put away. The storm rattled the roof and all craned their necks to look up.

"Yes, I was there, Cook. Sometimes it seems like a bad dream. Sometimes I wish I could forget."

Story-telling had to wait while the wild winds toyed with the roof timbers and cried through the shingles. Constant put a match to his pipe and drew deeply.

"Forty years ago. Ah, I was just a young man then. But I was much younger when I first went to work for my uncle Cyprien, to learn the log drives and how to handle timber in the mill ponds.

"Cyprien was a brutal man; very good at getting timber past rapids and running the camps but not a good man. If someone was sick or injured, my uncle gave them no mercy. Anyone who complained was sent home, or beaten to a pulp, for Cyprien was big and good with his fists.

"The nuns in Montreal sold a young lad, Indian Johnny we called him, to Cyprien as a slave; indentured they called it but it was near slavery. Johnny was one half Abenaki and he became an orphan when his parents were drowned. He was placed with the nuns and they sold him. Six years he had to serve, and Cyprien made certain he served full time.

"My uncle carried with him a silver whistle on a chain around his neck and he used it to control the men. He used it to mark the time to start work and when to quit. And he used it to torture Indian Johnny.

"Cyprien would whistle one short blast to mark day start or end. Two calls meant river-right; three was river-left. He did not need to yell to be understood with that whistle, but the men hated it; it sounded evil.

"When Cyprien had a chore for Johnny he would blow that whistle one long note, and god help Johnny if he did not respond at once. And Cyprien always had chores for the young lad. Any time of the day or night, my uncle would call Johnny with that whistle and Johnny would come running only to be slapped or made to go without a meal for reward.

"Sometimes the men would ask Johnny why he did not just slip away, get to another crew. But he would not. He was proud of his heritage and even though an orphan he would do nothing to disgrace the dignity of his forefathers. He would bear the beatings and work out his indenture.

"Indian Johnny and I became friends, for we were not far off in age. Sometimes when we talked, he told me of the spirits he worshipped, the way his father had taught him. He had to be very careful that Cyprien never saw him, but when Johnny had a little time to himself he prayed to the Windigo.

"He said the Windigo is the spirit of the storm; the spirit of the deep forests. He told me that the Windigo could protect those who were proud and brave, and would destroy any others in its path when it walked.

"But I did not really follow all what he said. Except that I did see that Indian Johnny was true to his indenture and brave in facing my uncle Cyprien.

"Then in the winter of '18 my uncle took me and Indian Johnny with him on a trip far up the St. Maurice River, way north in Quebec. At La Tuque he hired Jean Courteau as his guide and we headed out into the forest.

"All the way on that trip he used the whistle. There was no stopping until it blew, and he used it before the light was in the sky to get us to break camp. He made Indian Johnny carry a double pack and if he got more than a few steps behind, Cyprien blew that cursed whistle to make him hurry more.

"We travelled for two days straight; through the snow, across frozen lakes and steep hills on the east side of the St. Maurice. Beautiful country, and wild. Would have been a pleasant place; except for Cyprien.

"The third day on the trail, clouds closed in and the wind began to blow. By mid-afternoon the snow came thick and heavy, and it was not a night to spend in a lean-to; if there was a choice.

"Jean Courteau knew of a shelter a few miles farther on along the shore of a river. A place where the tribes sometimes met traders to exchange fur for steel, so there we headed.

"The darkness came early that afternoon and we pushed hard to keep ahead of the storm. Indian Johnny suffered badly, trying to keep up to Cyprien, Jean, and me, for he was carrying double weight and not yet even 17 years old."

Constant Palache paused in his recount while he re-lit his pipe. The storm outside was almost a continual cacophony, but everyone's attention was on the story.

"Keep going, Boss." Charbonneau said. "So what happened?"

Constant took a deep draw of his pipe and settled into his chair.

"Well we arrived at that camp, the CouCou Cache, Jean called it; on a bend in the river, just as night set in. It was not more than a rough log shack with dirt and sod for a roof, but it was solid and tight and had a fireplace.

"The storm blew like it does this night, maybe harder, and we could see no farther than our own feet. Cyprien made Indian Johnny search for wood to burn even though the lad was almost dead of fatigue. He did it though and we got that Cache warm.

"All might have gone well for we had food and shelter and Jean said we were no more than a one-day walk from Les Rapides Blanc – the destination we were headed for. Yet the way that storm blew we wondered if the old shack could stay standing. So we huddled around the fireplace and waited.

"As the place warmed up and uncle Cyprien loosened his jacket, all hell broke loose. He had lost his silver whistle. He searched through his overcoat and even his underwear, but no whistle.

"Cyprien went mad. He half tore the shack apart, and got young Johnny to empty all the packs on the floor, but still no whistle. My uncle paced the floor and would hear nothing about getting some food ready. Only that whistle mattered and he must find it.

"Jean and me, we tried to tell him he could get another as soon as we got to Quebec or Montreal, but he would hear nothing. That whistle was special; could not be re-made, and no other would do. That's when he started to blame Indian Johnny.

"The storm blew hard that night also lads, terrible hard, but when no sign of the whistle was found, Cyprien said it was all Johnny's fault the whistle had gone missing. Jean asked how that could be, since Johnny never touched le maudit sifflet. That made my uncle Cyprien real mad.

"Cyprien stood six-foot-six in his sock feet. When in a rage in a small room, it was something to behold. Like a crazed bull in a pen, he was, but still he had sense enough not to tackle Jean Courteau, and I was kin; so he cursed Indian Johnny.

"Nothing would do but Johnny must find that whistle, even if it was in the snow somewhere on our back trail. But lads, the night outside was not a place to be. Step outdoors and a man might never find the Cache again in the dark and drifts. Never mind that though. Indian Johnny must find the whistle and it had to be somewhere between here and our last camp.

"So Indian Johnny bundled up and headed out. Jean and me, we were feeling real bad for young Johnny. But my uncle said. "What good is being an Indian if he cannot track," and we watched him head out of the door.

"After he left, the storm got stronger and stronger until it seemed the roof would fly away. My uncle Cyprien just sat by the fire and stared and did not say another word. Me and Jean, we were hoping the best for Johnny out on such a night.

"But time went by and Johnny did not return. The storm

was making noises like it does tonight; almost like voices. Then it all went silent; like a tomb is silent. Not a sound. No wind, no voices, you could have heard a mouse walk if there were any.

"Cyprien, he went even madder in the silence. He stared around as if lost. It was then we heard the Windigo. Outside, from somewhere above the cabin, there came sobs as if a man in terrible sorrow. Then moaning and whimpers like someone in mortal pain, then shrieks of wild laughter.

"Then we heard the whistle! Louder than my uncle ever blew, it called in one long tone: the same tone Cyprien used to call Indian Johnny.

"Well my uncle Cyprien, when he heard that call, he jumped up so quick that me and Jean had to get out of his way. Then he just ran to the door and out into the storm. Nobody ever saw him again."

Constant Palache pushed back his chair and looked at his now-dead pipe, deciding not to re-light.

The cook broke the silence. "What happened to you and Jean, and Indian Johnny?"

Outside the storm was abating, the snow still falling heavy. Constant stretched and re-settled in his chair.

"When morning came, me and Jean found snowshoe tracks big as a double-bulk sleigh all round that CouCou Cache. Search as we might we saw no trace of Cyprien or even which direction he went. So we headed back to La Tuque and Quebec town."

It was O'Riley who asked. "And Indian Johnny, Constant? What became of him? Did he survive?"

"Johnny sent word that he is doing well. When he left the CouCou Cache he headed straight to Lac St. Jean where some of his kin live. He stays there now, and traps and hunts the moose."

Song of the Spirit River

The woodstove was stuffed full again, and quietly the men made their ways to the cots. Outside the snow stopped falling and the wind died away. One by one, stars filled the spaces left in the sky by departing clouds.

Long before dawn, the cook had the table piled high with pan bread, molasses and bacon fat. The aroma of coffee filled the air.

Charbonneau, the teamster, was the first to open the door; anxious to check on his horses. But he had only pushed his way a short distance through the drifted snow when he called. "Hey Boss, you men, come see!"

From where he stood, a trail of footprints was plain in the fresh-fallen snow. Deep and wide they were, heading right off into the forest. And there, hanging on a peg by the cabin door, was an antique silver whistle.

Constant Palache pocketed the whistle and later that day, as he was leaving for a shanty over in Avoca, he took the time to stand on the edge of La Belle's Falls. With the late winter sun shining bright, and where the open river drops over sheer rock, he stood and thought of his uncle Cyprien and Indian Johnny and the CouCou Cache.

Then he tossed the whistle into the water and went on his way.

The CouCou Cache was situated on the Windigo River, a short distance from where that river ran into the St. Maurice in the district of La Mauricie, Quebec. Who built it or when is lost to history. It was used as a Hudson's Bay trading post from 1875 to 1913; though it is known to have existed long before that.

In 1938 an electrical power dam was constructed on the St. Maurice River and the site of the old CouCou Cache is now beneath the waters of Le Reservoir Blanc.

Two hundred years ago the backwoods north of Gren-ville, Quebec, were almost completely uninhabited. It is known that there was a community of Scots and Irish living near and around what is now called McGillivray Lake before 1810. At that time only the most adventurous of souls lived further beyond; far flung and independent.
To the north of McGillivray Lake, past the modern commu-nity of Kilmar and into the southern region of Harrington, there is a lovely valley dominated on the southwest by a mountain named the Highlands.
On a hillside off to the northeast of the Highlands is an-other high spot which slopes gently down to the south. There was a meadow on this hillside which for some rea-son never grew trees; an open place in a closed-in land, where the view stretches far out over the lower hills.
A passer-through in long-ago times stopped to look, and the name he gave that location stayed for generations; after one woman and one man made the place their home.

Big Lonely

The cabin was in deep silence as Jim McRae lay sleepless in his bed. Beside him, his wife Nora snuggled up a little closer then relaxed into dreams. In the light beam from the near-full moon he could see the wall clock reading past midnight.

He looked at his wife's face, soft in sleep, and won-dered how he was so fortunate as to have found Nora. Without her assurances that he was capable, he would never have acquired Big Lonely.

The old clock ticked and the cabin started to take on a

chill from the cold winter night. It was December 21, 1831; ten years and three months since he set foot on the dock at Montreal. A shiver went through Jim; not from the cold but the memories of that landing.

He had got on board the emigrant ship to Canada from Greenock Scotland with his mother, father, and younger sister. Only he debarked. Ship fever set in about six weeks out of port. His mother, already weakened by sea-sickness, died first. Then his sister about one week later, followed by his father only three days before he landed in Quebec. The port authorities confiscated all his family's goods leaving him with only enough clothes to cover his back and completely alone when he finally arrived at Montreal.

Mabel MacLeod had seen him that day, standing lost on the dock, and she took him under her wing and back with her to the MacLeod settlement in Glengarry. There he lived in her cabin and worked in her fields. There he learned to read and write, to use an axe and plough a furrow. Mabel's nephew, Norman MacLeod, took him as a helper when constructing log cabins and that gave him experience at building.

It was Big Norman who brought him along on a trip to the Hamilton sawmill just above the rapids on the Ottawa River, an excursion which set him to dreaming. Across the river stood some buildings along the shore and behind them rose high hills.

Those hills standing tall and green in the summer sun stayed in Jim's mind long after he returned to the MacLeod settlement, as did the image of the bustling activity surrounding the sawmill. He questioned Norman about what lay beyond those high hills as they worked squaring timbers for another house. But Norman had not gone farther than the top of the Grenville canal. So Jim was left with only a vision until Constant Palache rode in on horseback, and his world opened up quicker than he could have imagined.

The clock ticked away in the silence. Jim pulled Nora a little closer in the warm bed, but memories unfolded and he let them float back.

When Jim saw Constant coming into the settlement from the Cornwall road, then swinging off his horse to greet McGillivray the blacksmith, he knew he was looking at a special person. Later that night, when a group had sat around MacCuaig's table and pipes were lighted, Norman mentioned to Constant Palache Jim's curiousness about what lay beyond the hills at Grenville. One answer led to another, then questions about news from the immigrant settlements which were forming in the valleys of Argenteuil. Constant travelled that region and seemed to know it all.

The next morning after Jim had done his chores, he saw Constant Palache at the blacksmith's shop conversing with Norman. Then they called him over. Constant was heading up into the hills along the Rouge River and needed a good assistant. So he packed a bag with his few belongings, said farewell to Mabel, Norman, and all the others who had welcomed him, and swung up behind Constant Palache for the life changing ride to the river; and to Big Lonely.

He fell asleep with pleasant thoughts of his friend Constant Palache: Voyageur and paddler for the Hudson's Bay Company. Timber scout and outback man supreme.

Nora shifted and awoke slightly. Just enough to look over towards the shadows nearer to the wood stove, for Jim and her were not alone in the cabin on Big Lonely.

In a smaller bed with high wooden sides slept Mandy Ann.
Four years, five months old. Mandy Ann had been born
south of Big Lonely in that little community in the valley
north of Grenville. After assuring herself that the girl slept
soundly, Nora snuggled closer to Jim's strong warm back
and went over her journey to life on Big Lonely.

Nora Patton was her name before she married Jim.
She was born in St. Andrews East into a big happy family where her mother taught her to sew and cook and the
many tricks required to run a smooth household. At sixteen
she took a job working for the MacMillan's in their fine
stone home at Grenville, right across the river from the
Hamilton's.

Her attractive appearance, gentle manners, and ability to set a table made her a vital part of the MacMillan
household. There, over the feasts she helped present and
the spirits she poured, gathered colourful crowds of entre-
preneurs, ladies of high fashion, and travellers from many
places. There she met Constant Palache and Constant
introduced her to Jim McRae. Now she lay here with him,
with their child sleeping close, and wished for little more.

During the two and one half years she worked for the
MacMillan family, she had met many of the officers sta-
tioned at Grenville. At the grand gatherings which Mrs.
MacMillan enjoyed putting together, her ability to engage
conversation sometimes found her in the company of gen-
tlemen lonely for a young woman's presence. Her days off
were often filled with gay rides in carriages, on horseback,
or even in canoes with strong intelligent men; but none
compared to Jim.

She met him while he was with Constant Palache in
Grenville, working for a man named McCallum, checking
a site for a sawmill. Jim was twenty years old when they

met. From the first introduction at the MacMillan house, they got along. She could never quite describe it to herself but he seemed to be the other half of her. They could see each other across a room and sense each other's thoughts. Feel the same flow of life as they made small talk and walked along the canal. When he left with Constant for a trek far to the north, she knew he would be back.

Jim did return in the spring. He came to the MacMillan house asking for her, informing Mrs. MacMillan of his wish to court Nora. Mrs. MacMillan made no objection whatsoever for when she saw the shine in Nora's eyes at the request she was wise enough to step aside.

Jim and Nora spent the early summer making plans. Where they would live at the start, how they would make their living, where they would carve out their place in the area, which was expanding rapidly. They were married by the Anglican minister in Grenville on Saturday, August 1, 1826.

The old wall clock ticked, the moon beams grew longer and the cabin submitted to the 30-below winter night.

Jim's eyes opened with the first gray light of dawn showing through frosted glass. Nora still slumbered, deep in her blankets. There was a hard chill in the cabin as he arose and quickly dressed. He went to the wood stove and stacked in birch bark, cedar kindling and dry strips of hardwood and struck a match. He closed the stove door as the flames caught quickly, then walked to the window to look out at the pale dawn.

As the stove heated and spread its warmth across the single room, Jim's attention was taken by a little head, all surrounded by tussled curly blonde locks, popping out of patchwork quilts. Mandy Ann sat up in her crib, wrapped in her quilts, and spoke to her father.

"Oh Poppy, is it Christmas yet?" she asked while yawning deeply. Jim just shook his head. "No Mandy, not for a few more days." A slight frown crossed his face for he knew she was looking forward to that day and he was ill prepared.

Little Mandy Ann twisted the quilt in her hands and talked downwards. "Sandy Claus will find me up here, won't he Poppy? Like he did at Granny Rourke's house, won't he Poppy? He will know where I live?"

Across the room Nora was awake, lying with her head propped on her arm and listening to her child's banter. Her eyes met Jim's and they both knew each other's thoughts. Mandy Ann had been born in the cabin along the Scotch Road and Christmas in that community had been special.

Granny Rourke, that wonderful widow who had taught Nora so much of backwoods life, had introduced Mandy Ann to the idea of Santa Claus; the old wise man who gave gifts to good girls and boys. Jim and Nora took on the custom and each year on Christmas morning there had been a special treat, from Santa Claus. But up here on Big Lonely they were at a loss as to what they could give to keep the tradition alive.

Nora spoke softly. "Oh Mandy Ann. This is our first Christmas up here and Santa Claus might not find you right away. He will be busy down at the settlements, and you don't want him to miss all those girls and boys while he looks for you way up here. Do you?"

"Sandy Claus will find me. I know he will. Sandy Claus knows where all the good girls live. Granny told me so. You will see, Mommy. Sandy Claus will..." Her words trailed off as she glanced from her mother to her Dad.

Jim trimmed off the damper on the stove and thought

of Christmas. He should have been more prepared for
Mandy Ann's first Christmas on Big Lonely. Down on the
Scotch, it had been simple and fun to make up the idea
of Santa Claus. When he went to town in September he
should have picked something for her, but he did not and
now Christmas Eve was four days away.

The air in the cabin warmed quickly as the sides of the
wood stove took on a dull glow. Nora was at the table mix-
ing buckwheat flour, eggs and milk for pancakes. Little
Mandy Ann sat on a stool with her doll, telling it of Sandy
Claus and how he found children everywhere. Granny
said so.

Jim definitely did not want Mandy Ann's innocence to
be shattered, nor did Nora. When breakfast was finished
and they stood close while cleaning dishes, Nora asked.
"She is so looking forward to Christmas, Jim. What can
we do to keep it special?"

Jim had been considering that same question all
through breakfast and he had only one solution. "I'll go
to town. I've been thinking three days gone. Will you be
alright here alone? I'll see to it that the hay is down and
plenty of wood in. Leave tomorrow morning; one day
down, one day back, a few hours to stop and rest and see
Granny. Should be back in the late afternoon, the 24th."

Nora nodded assent.

Jim spent that day getting ready for the trek. He and
Nora had three cows, (two dry), and a young bull they
were hoping would build a herd of good Jerseys. They
shared the cozy barn with three pigs, one sturdy Canadian horse, and eight chickens in a coup. He made certain
there was enough hay down from the mow and water from
the spring to last until his return.

The next morning dawned clear and cold. As the sun

broke the eastern horizon, Jim laced on his cowhide moccasins, donned his heavy woollen coat and hat, hugged
Mandy Ann and kissed Nora good bye, then headed out
on snowshoes for the 20-mile walk to Grenville. Nora held
Mandy Ann in her arms at the doorway as they watched
him go.

To some, 20 miles cross-country through the backwoods
in the dead of winter might seem daunting. But after
all the days and nights he had tromped beside Constant
Palache, learning to read the land and know the wildlife,
Jim was more than ready for the walk.

He headed down from his cabin on Big Lonely; down
that long gentle slope which had first drawn his attention
to this place, mapping the trail in his mind. Beyond the
edge of his meadow, through some pines and he would
turn left. There was a join in the trail here; a sharp right
would take him north, to the Rouge if he went far enough.
But he had no interest there now. He would take the left,
then straight for about five miles where he would skirt a
lake. Beyond that it was through the forest to the top of the
Scotch Road, then the relatively easy walk: the ten miles to
Grenville. As he walked, he remembered his first passage
this way, and Constant Palache.

After he left Mabel MacLeod's farm, he had wandered
far with Constant, packing gear and taking notes. Constant was completely at home in the wild, finding food and
shelter wherever he was, no matter what season; and he
taught Jim the ways of the wild: how to make a camp, fix a
snowshoe or repair a canoe; how to mimic the bellow of the
moose, how to understand the call of the wolf. For the best
part of three years, Jim had lived beside Constant, learning
and trying to emanate the man. They had walked the forests from the Gatineau River to Morin Bottoms, from Raw

Song of the Spirit River

Cliff to Mont Tremblant.

It was on an exploration to some highlands, about three miles distant from where his cabin sits now, when he looked out to the east and saw what Constant called Big Lonely. It was the south face of a sloping hill where no trees grew. It appeared to Jim when he first sighted it as a meadow ready for the plough.

On his request, he and Constant had hiked over to the top of that slope and looked over to the heights where they had stood two hours before. There as he looked out he understood why Constant Palache had named this place Big Lonely.

They camped that night on the meadow and Jim explored. He found that there were many good maple trees for sugar and potash. Right where he thought a cabin could sit was a stand of big cedar trees, and amazingly for this height, a spring flowed with fine water. The sun set beyond the distant highlands and rose the next day with a blaze of splendour over the lower hills to the east. The place was big, with a vista almost unmatched by anything Jim had ever seen. And god, it was lonely; made a man seem small when looking out. Big Lonely it was and he would live here; the vision never left him.

Jim tromped through the snow, well on his way to town on a fine winter's day.

Back on Big Lonely, Nora and Mandy Ann had chores galore. Together they fed the stock and brought the horse out to exercise in the snow. The sun shone bright and even though the thermometer read twenty below, the sun made the front yard pleasant. Then they went inside and spent the rest of the morning learning ABC's, Mandy Ann concentrating hard as she traced out the letters.

When they were finished lunch, Nora decided to make soap; she was getting short and had all ingredients needed. She got the stove hot and put slabs of fat from the hog they had butchered into a big iron pot and set it to render. Mandy Ann watched closely as her mother worked, and Nora explained every move she did in the process and why it was done, and remembered her journey to Big Lonely.

After their wedding, Jim had brought her up the Scotch Road to McGillivray's lake where there was a community. Jim had leased a log cabin there, backed onto a little stream, with a garden space already planted. Only about a mile north lived Granny Rourke and that first year while Jim worked in the forests, Nora spent much of her spare time with Granny.

Granny Rourke - Mildred - if one wished to be formal, had grown up in the backwoods, been married and had children. Her children both died from a fever she could not control, then her husband was killed when a tree fell on him while logging. Despite this, Granny lived on and held a positive attitude and a solid faith in God. Over sixty when Nora first met her, Granny Rourke became a mentor for Nora, showing her the many and varied wisdoms needed to run a backwoods household.

Nora had made soap before she met Granny, but Granny showed her how to do it without lye purchased from a store. She taught Nora how to find the edible plants and where the ginseng and wild hops grow. She showed her how to smoke and salt meats to make them last, and how to whip an old apple tree into sprouting new blossoms. Lessons learned from a lifetime of pioneer living, Granny passed on to Nora.

In the autumn of their second year married, after Jim had returned from an excursion with Constant Palache,

he had packed a bag with some supplies and they went
walking; straight north for a distance, then a big swing
around a lake which shimmered and reflected in the fall
sunshine. They continued, after stopping to eat a bite,
walking through old forests on a trail that followed the
low lands heading almost straight north. Then at a fork in
the trail, Jim turned right. He took her by a devious trip
up a long hill and then to the left to exit the woods at the
heights of Big Lonely, looking down at the swooping vis-
tas of far-away hills that rolled away to the south. There,
right near some ancient cedars, near the bubbling spring,
Jim made a bush camp for her and him.

He took saplings to form a dome and slabs of bark
from downed trees to cover and make shelter. Then he
cut cedar boughs to make a bed and spread out blankets.
After a meal and tea they watched the sun set beyond
the highlands, then made love the whole night through.
When the sun rose in the morning and she saw Big Lonely
in the light of dawn, she, like Jim, knew she had found
her home. The place they would make their stand against
all which life might throw at them.

As the day wore on, Jim was at the big valley at the
north end of the Scotch Road. From here, the next ten
miles were fairly easy going, for there was a broken trail.
He stopped at Granny Rourke's cottage to say hello and
explain his need for a gift for Mandy Ann. He had thought
of going straight to town, but a look at Granny's roof
showed it needed to be shovelled clear. So, while Granny
strapped on her snowshoes and went off to see the Algonquin woman who made leather items, Jim shovelled.

Granny came back late. Jim had cleared all her roofs
and it was dark so he stayed the night. The next day

he was up early and jog-trotted on his snowshoes down to Grenville and the general store. When he arrived mid-morning, the clerk told him that if he could just wait a bit, the owner would be coming up from Cushing with a fresh load of goods. So Jim hung around.

He talked to Mr. and Mrs. MacMillan, telling that Nora and child were well in their home. Then he sat in Leroy's tavern and heard about who was hiring and who had won the great fight the night before. It was almost four in the afternoon before Mr. Wilson arrived with a sleigh full. Jim chose two rolls of calico, different colours, thread, needles, and some lace. Then he purchased fifty pounds of flour, ten pounds of salt, five pounds of cane sugar, some yeast, a big bag of coloured candy, and a kaleidoscope.

When he was wrapping up his goods the store owner opened a crate to show him a gun he had brought for sale: a double-barrel coach gun, twenty balls to the pound, percussion cap fired. He and Jim went out behind the store as the owner demonstrated how there was no hang-fire with percussion caps. Jim bought the gun on the whim; complete with powder, five pounds of lead balls and caps.

He spent that night in a cot above the tavern and before daylight he was on his way up the Scotch, carrying about ninety pounds on his back. But he had carried double this weight sometimes when travelling with Constant Palache; the day dawned clear and the trail was good.

Up beyond McGillivray's lake at Granny's cabin she was waiting for him. The Algonquin woman had delivered a wonderfully-made doll. All soft doeskin and beads, with corn husks plaited for hair. She insisted that Jim stay for a bite, and he found her back door needed fixing, so it was mid-afternoon before he set off on the last part of his walk back to Big Lonely.

Song of the Spirit River

Nora started her day early also, feeding the animals while she listened to Mandy Ann's chatter. They were both looking forward to Jim's return, figuring him to arrive about time for supper. He would be tired; she knew that, so she would make something light and have a big meal on Christmas day. She had been hoarding for the day and she began the preparations.

She took out a smoked ham she had set carefully away then chose her best squash and turnip. Onions and potatoes would be trimmed up just before the meal tomorrow, and there were jarred wild plums for dessert. Tonight she would serve him flatbread and soup and tea.

She gave Mandy Ann her lessons and as the day wore on, she exercised the horse and thought of her love for Jim and this place, Big Lonely. She gave Mandy Ann an early supper, thinking to wait for Jim and eat with him.

As the sun was setting low and her lamp lit on the table, Nora smiled at the thought of Jim's return. He would be tired for certain, but she was not. She stepped outside of her door and looked down over the meadows. The full moon would be rising soon, for she could see its light starting to colour the eastern sky. At least Jim would not be in darkness, but she had no fear for him. He had learned from Constant Palache.

In the last bit of daylight she took her buckets to the stoned-in spring and filled them, splashing water on the edge of spring. "Have to be careful," she thought, as she carried those two buckets to the house to be warmed for her and Jim's bath. "That's going to get slippery."

She got the stove burning strong and placed a large pot to heat while she put Mandy Ann in her crib. Mandy was nowhere ready for sleep until her Poppy arrived, so she sat in her bed and watched her mother putter away the time.

Nora had a plan: When Jim arrived she would feed him, then bathe him, pull the drapes around their bed and caress him until he slept. She smiled to herself at the thought of her man's power and what sometimes happened when she teased him just beyond his control. She checked the water on the stove; two more buckets would make a great bath.

On the trail, Jim had about five miles left to go. It was hard slogging with the load he carried, even though he had made trail just two days ago. There was a crust which when he broke through, made him lift his snowshoes high for each step. When he started the long skirt around the lake he paused to look around and listen.

All was still in the forest of tall hardwoods, the moon beginning to mottle the path in bright light and shadows. He would be back at Big Lonely a couple of hours late but he would get there and the thought of Mandy Ann's shining face and Nora's soft body waiting for him quickened his steps.

As the moon rose over Big Lonely, Nora tucked Mandy Ann into her covers and added wood to the fire. Jim was late but should be here soon; meanwhile her water was evaporating away. Two more buckets.

While Mandy Ann lay talking to her doll, Nora put on her boots and coat, picked up her buckets, and went out into the cold night air. It was gorgeous, the moon part way up lighting the snow covered meadow in a golden light. She set the buckets aside while she checked all the stock in the steamy stable. Then she went to the spring for water.

Song of the Spirit River

As she picked up the full buckets and started towards the cabin her feet went out from under her on the sloped ice and she fell backwards, whiplashing her head onto the rock-hard surface. She lay dazed, unable to move a muscle.

She must have lost consciousness, for when she came to the moon was higher and she was very cold. She half crawled her way back to the cabin and into the warm space. She sat on a chair but started to pass out so she went to her bed.

Mandy Ann watched her mother with great concern. She knew something was very wrong but not what it was. She heard her mother saying to stay in bed until Poppy came back, then saw her mother slump onto the bed without another word. Something was terribly wrong with Mommy.

Mandy Ann did as she was told and stayed in her crib, watching and hoping her mother would awaken. But she did not. When the stove began to cool down and Mommy still had not got up to add wood, Mandy Ann climbed out of her bed and went to her mother. She shook her gently with no results then called, "Mommy... Mommy!" No answer.

Mandy Ann was only four and a half, but she had the clear head of a pioneer child. Her mother was sleeping hard and would not awake, but Poppy would be home soon and he would make things right. She looked at the wall clock; nine and three-quarters time.

Maybe she could go and meet him on the trail. Get him to hurry a little bit. She opened the cabin door to look down the meadow but no sign of Poppy. Mandy Ann went over to her mother's bed and called gently again but Mommy slept soundly.

She considered the stove which was almost out, but knew she was not to touch it. She sat on her stool and thought for awhile, then put on her warm winter wear, and after a last shake of her mother's shoulder, stepped out into the moonlit night.

She did not go far from the cabin for a while after quietly closing the door behind her. She just stood there and took in the silence and the golden light which lit the meadow and the barn and made the far away forest sparkle. From out of that forest her Poppy would come walking soon so she just stomped around in the snow to keep her feet warm and waited.

But the snowshoe tracks Poppy had left in the shining snow, leading down the gentle slope of the meadow, beckoned her and she followed them with tentative steps. She did not intend to go far but the walking was easy, for with her light weight she did not sink beyond the crust; leaving tiny tracks in the snow alongside those of her father.

The moon was right overhead and the whole countryside shone nearly as bright as a sunny day. She continued on downwards, not worried about being out alone, for she knew Poppy would walk out of the dark forest at the bottom of the meadow. Then she would tell him about Mommy, and he would make it right.

By the time she reached the bottom end of the meadow, the big trees seemed to open up for her and signs of snowshoe tracks led straight ahead. Mandy Ann looked back up the long slope to the cabin. She could see it clearly in the moonlight and it looked like a doll house way up there, with a glimmer of light in the window and the moon casting a slight shadow. All was silent as she entered beneath the tall trees and hurried, just a bit, to a long narrow opening in the woods.

Song of the Spirit River

She could still make out the dim outline of snowshoes leading straight out ahead, but there was no sign of Poppy. Indecision came upon her and she began to think maybe she had gone too far. But she walked on a bit more, hoping desperately to see Poppy appear out of those distant shadows.

Then she decided she was too far. From where she stood there was nothing familiar; only the white snow and dark trees lining both sides of the trail. A slight shock of fear ran through Mandy Ann. She would go back to Mommy and wait there. But when she turned around, the slight fear turned to near panic at what she saw.

The moon, no longer directly overhead, was casting shadows so that while going forward was bright moonlight, she now faced nearly pitch-black. She could not make out the snowshoe tracks in the darkness between the trees and in her attempt to hurry, missed the right side trail towards her home and got on the little-used left path, leading to nothing but a logging shanty far up the Rouge.

When her walking took her farther into the shadows and nothing looked right, Mandy Ann tried to keep her mind clear; figuring she could not be that far off, she kept going straight ahead. Then she heard the wolf.

Jim McRae was only about a mile from home when he heard the wolf's call. He stopped to listen, for in that silence the howl rang clear off the side of the highlands. Jim had no real fear of wolves. He and Constant had many experiences with the big timber wolves which roamed these forests. But nevertheless, there was something very primordial in the call for the pack; and he knew that was what this lone wolf was doing.

"None of my affairs," he thought as he straightened his pack and continued on the last stretch before the turn up the hill. When he heard the second wolf call from some distance ahead, on what he calculated was the trail up to the Rouge, he paused again. Constant Palache had taught Jim how to read the wolf's call so he was not surprised when he heard the third wolf howl from the deep forest well ahead. A pack was forming.

Jim had only gone a short distance farther when he heard the fourth wolf sing. He knew how they talked: the first wolf found something of interest, then she called her family, then they would join up to see if the quarry was worth the fight. Likely, the victim was something old or wounded which would require little effort for four wolves. He tromped on.

Mandy Ann was almost in full-blown panic. She had never seen a wolf but that howl she heard made her hair stand up and sent shivers of fear through her little body. She saw a clear place of moonlight ahead and tried to run to it but she sank in the snow and heard the second wolf, ahead and to the left.

She took her time now, stepping carefully, aiming for the light, hearing the third wolf call, desperately hoping to gain the bottom of her meadow. But when she did reach open ground it was flatland with a deep gully dividing it and blocking her passage.

Then she heard the fourth wolf yelp from what seemed directly behind her and she ran once more; to the edge of the gully and slid down. The last thing she saw before slipping low was a large dark form watching her slide, not fifty feet away.

Song of the Spirit River

Jim was just at the point where the trail split, heading up out of the forest and beyond to his meadow, when he saw a shadow moving between tree trunks off to his left. Only a quarter mile to go now and he would be heading into his yard and the welcoming arms of Nora and Mandy Ann.

Those wolves had him thinking. Whatever they were after was not far ahead, maybe a half mile or so. Jim McRae knew the cycle of life in the backwoods and felt no disdain for wolves. They kept the rest of nature healthy, weeding out the weak, sick, and old. Yet good winter wolf pelts were valuable items and here were some which might be had.

His cabin could wait for a little bit more; he was almost home. He would check out those wolves, maybe bag one or two if the situation was right.

He removed his 90-pound pack and set it carefully under a tree, then unlimbered the coach gun. He carefully checked to be certain the caps were well seated, as he had been instructed; he knew each barrel held one twenty gauge slug.

He took off his snowshoes, loosened his jacket, and removed his hat so as to miss no sounds. With his trail hatchet under his belt and the new coach gun held in front, Jim McRae melted into the forest shadows.

Mandy Ann's panic had gone away, or mostly. Although not quite five, the spirit of pioneer life flowed strong; she looked around her new surroundings.

In the moonlight she could see that it was a gully with a little stream at the bottom. The stream was frozen solid now but at some point it had risen high and cut a section of the gully bank, leaving an overhang and a place just large enough for her to crawl in. She got herself in there with her back pressed deep into the earth and waited.

She did not have to wait long before she saw the first wolf jump off the bank onto the frozen ice just a short distance away. Then she saw some snow slide down from where another beast stood almost right above her. Two more joined the first on the ice and began to approach.

When they were only about fifty feet away, she tried to scream but found that her voice did not work and only a whimper came out. With three great timber wolves now very near to where she was backed into the earth bank, she took off one of her bead-embroidered mittens and threw it at them. The wolves jumped back in surprise but did not go far.

Jim was coming from the way Mandy Ann had run, towards the gully he knew was there, but from a different angle. He was using all the skills taught to him by Constant Palache, creeping so cautiously in his moccasins that the wolves were totally unaware of the hunters becoming the hunted.

Jim snuck closer. He saw the wolves close in then scatter, and knew pretty well where their prey was hiding. He had no idea of what it was they were after, nor did he care; it was hides he wanted, then get home.

There were four wolves intent on something and Jim McRae only had two balls in his coach gun. He watched and reconsidered as a fifth wolf joined the pack.

Mandy Ann was in trouble and she knew it. But she did not panic a second time; certain in the way of young things that she was strong and all would work out. When those great dark shapes had inched so close she could almost feel their breath, she threw her second mitten and once more the pack backed off, but only a few feet.

Jim saw the fifth wolf come along the gully bed, but it, like the others was intent on the quarry under the bank and was completely unaware of Jim's presence. With that many big timber wolves, they might put up a stand; and he wanted a pelt or two, not a fight. So he was beginning to slip away when he saw the wolf pack jump and something land on the ground in front of them. Then he watched as they crept closer again.

This was Mandy Ann's last stand. She had nothing left to throw and the creatures were no longer afraid; edging closer. She calmed her mind, let a big picture of her happy home fill her thoughts, took a large inhale and yelled. "Poppy!"And her voice worked.

Within an instant Jim McRae was over the gully bank, between Mandy Ann and the pack. He fired twice then used the gun butt as a club until it shattered. He split a black skull with his hatchet and broke another beast's back as it tried to scramble up the bank.

As suddenly as it had began the battle was over. Jim dropped his hatchet and grasped Mandy Ann tight to him as she sobbed. "Poppy. Oh Poppy! I knew you would come."

As Jim carried Mandy Ann back to where his goods were stashed, she recounted to him what happened to her Mommy and why she wanted to meet him on the trail and how she got lost.

"All is good, Mandy Ann." Jim said gently to his daughter as he shouldered his pack and lifted her into his arms. "You are brave and you did what you thought should be done. No one could ask for more. Let's go see how Mommy is doing." Jim's long strides took them up across the meadow in the misty shaded moonlight, to the cabin on Big Lonely.

Nora recovered from the concussion and although she had a massive headache, that Christmas was one of the happiest days of her life. When Mandy Ann awoke Christmas morning and found the kaleidoscope and doll, she reprimanded Mommy for not believing Sandy Claus could locate her; even out here beyond the settlements.

Jim explained about finding Mandy Ann and bagging some wolves, but never told how close the situation had been.

They lived up there on Big Lonely for much of their lives. Over the years, their family grew to five children. Nora and Jim McRae watched from their heights as the land below them changed and the Harrington valley was born. The trails they blazed took on names and became roads: Rouge River, Harrington and Kilmar. Forests were felled and prosperous farms appeared.

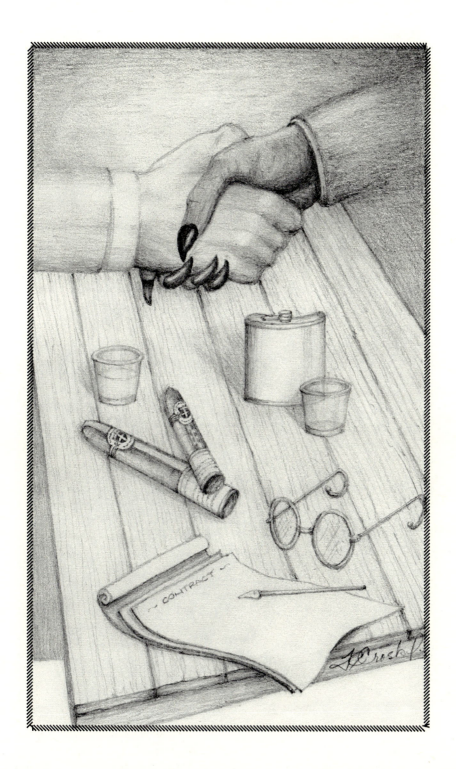

The Devil and Barry Water

I was sitting on my porch one sunny summer afternoon, on the old farm I bought in what they now call Grenville-sur-la-Rouge Township in western Quebec.

A nice old place, but the land has not been turned in a long time. Never mattered much to me, for I just bought the property as a getaway. My grandparents had lived around here back in the early part of the 1900's so there is a bit of family connection; never thought too much about it.

Anyway, I was just sitting there, thinking I should be doing something other than sitting but it was such a fine afternoon; the kind of day to sit and think and watch the clouds go by.

There are not too many cars driving by my old farm, and that is one of the main reasons I got it. Besides, the roads are so bad that pretty well the only folk on this stretch are locals. Not many of them either: Old Charlie lives down aways. And Jerome's laneway is about half a mile before mine.

So I was sitting thinking about all the work I wasn't going to do when a car pulled into my drive. The lane is long, and sometimes tourists just use it as a place to turn around when they are lost. But this car didn't turn; it just came up my long driveway, slow and easy.

I was thinking to myself, "Here's another lost soul. Tell the good folk how to get back to civilization. Then go back to watching the clouds," though there were few.

A really nice black BMW seven series pulled up in

front of my porch and shut off the engine. First I was feeling kind of sorry for some city slicker lost up here, fearing his nice car would fall into a pothole.

The door opened and a well-dressed man stepped out looking like he had just come off a relaxing Caribbean cruise then checked out my old farm.

I immediately thought it must be a municipal inspector of some kind. There are lots of them around and that's the type of vehicle they drive.

But he did not hold up a badge or start taking pictures, so I relaxed a bit. When he closed the car door and came towards my steps I went back to the lost tourist idea, for he seemed friendly; not like those inspectors.

"Barry Water is my name," he said.

"Just took a drive up the laneway to see how the old place looks. Don't mean to bother you, son. Only stay a minute."

So while he stood and checked out the brush and trees, I was looking him over. His face looked like the man on a Mexican beer commercial; all tanned with a beard well trimmed and bright eyed.

I pretty sure he was not an inspector of any kind by now, and he seemed to be familiar with the surroundings so not a lost tourist either.

"Got relatives around here?" I asked. "Know the country a bit?"

"Used to live here," he replied.

"Know the country well. No farms left like in my day, but the hills are the same and I thought I'd come and see. While I'm in the neighbourhood."

I like to learn about folk in these hills. I know my grandparents had a farm somewhere long ago, but I miss some of the older names, and I thought to myself, "Here is a chance to learn, pick his brains before he heads off."

So I asked, "When were you here? You had a spot somewhere around?"

Barry Water walked away from his shiny BMW to stand at the bottom of my porch. From close up, his eyes were blue and had what looked like a permanent bit of smile. Nice looking man and relaxed.

"I lived in this very house," he said.

"Moved out in the summer of '12. Before that, I lived in a cabin back up in the hills aways."

When he said '12, I was thinking either he had his dates mixed up or maybe I should be calling one of those municipal inspectors; for this was 2016 and when I bought the place it had been abandoned and run down.

So I asked him while he stood there looking like he was a taking a walk down memory lane, "You moved out not long before I got here in '15."

Barry looked at me with his twinkling eyes, and walked up the steps and put out his hand.

"Bartholomew H. Water", he said and put out a tanned hand to shake.

"To whom have I the pleasure of speaking?"

"Gord Fraser." I said.

"Pleased to meet you, Bartholomew."

"Call me Barry. Always liked that name better."

Barry was still looking around, though he was relaxed and not like the kind of man who would be confused, so I said. "Take a chair for a minute, Barry? Take a load off?"

So Barry Water and I sat and looked at the clouds for a while, and I figured it was a good time to set his dates straight so I said. "The place must have been a bit run down when you were here Barry?"

We were both looking over towards the shiny seven

series.

Barry glanced at me with an odd look but changed the subject.

"You have any relatives around, Gord? What brought you here?"

I told him that my grandparents had a farm not far away. Nothing left of the farm now, but there are a couple of lots divided and houses there, I told him. It got me thinking of my grandparents.

Arthur Fraser was my grandfather's name, though my dad had moved to the city and I grew up there. Never knew my grandparents well – not sure why.

That was partly what got me interested in buying a place back here, to see a little bit of the old country.

But while sitting on the porch watching clouds with Barry Water, I thought to myself, "Water is a familiar name, somehow." And in thinking, it occurred to me that my grandmother's maiden name was Water, I said to Barry.

"Just wanted a place out of the way, so to speak. Some good spot to sit and think, like today.

"Never knew my grandparents much, though now that you mention the name, Water was my grandmother's name before she married, Grandma Sarah I think but I'm not certain."

Barry Water stopped staring off into the distance to look at me, then stared over the farm for a while before he said.

"Important to know where you come from, Gord. I think of all the people who once lived around here every time I come back. But I don't come around as often as I used to."

I looked at Barry Water as he took off his panama hat and laid it on the table between us. He certainly did not look like a nut case, sitting there in a light summer jacket that probably cost more than my truck.

Certainly no glazed-over eyes with him. No sir. His eyes looked like they'd seen some things. Full head of dark hair too; kind of hard to tell if he was 60 or 35. Barry did not look like the kind of man who would live in a dump.

So I took the subject back to when I moved in and how the roof had leaked in places. Someone had taken the banister and the iron floor grates.

"Must have been in rough shape when you moved out in '12." I said to Barry Water.

Barry studied me for a moment then said, "Actually it was in fine shape when I decided to move around a bit, see the world.

"Better let you get on with your day, Gord Fraser, but it is still a nice place to sit. And a fine day for sitting."

He was about to get up and put on his panama hat that probably cost more than my garage, when he settled back a bit.

"You said your grandmother's name was Water. Do you know what her first name was? I kind of like to keep track of my relatives, though most are gone now. Wouldn't have been Sarah Jane, was it?"

Sarah was her first name, that I knew, and Water is an unusual name in these parts, so I gave up on the mixed up dates for a time.

Barry Water did not look any older than me and maybe younger, so I asked him, if he had a moment – we could see if there was a family connection.

It was nice on the porch, so Barry settled back into his seat and looked me over long and hard. He set the panama back on the table and said.

"Gord, if your grandmother's maiden name was Sarah Jane Water, then that would make us relations.

"The last of mine around here maybe, and it is curious that you took the place. But no matter.

"The way I see it, Gord, is we got two choices on what to do with the rest of this afternoon. I go and do something else for awhile, let you get on with your day; or we can sit a spell and I'll sort out some dates and tell a story. We are kin and it's all history now.

"Your choice."

It was a nice sunny day and there were not many clouds to watch. Barry still reminded me of that commercial for Mexican beer, of which I had a few bottles inside, so I asked if he would like one and he said yes.

"It's a bit of long tale, Gord," he said.

I told him there was no place to go in a hurry and he agreed. Barry asked me if I minded if he smoked and I said no. As he reached into the breast pocket of that nice jacket he asked, "You smoke Gord? Enjoy a cigar now and then?"

I remembered a cigar I smoked when I was a kid. Made me turn green, literally, and since then I have puffed on a few. I know a little bit about cigars and even bought one for fifty American on a trip to the Dominican one time.

"Want to try one of these?" Barry Water asked as he pulled out two strange-looking cigars marked King of Denmark.

"Some people don't like the odd colour." Barry said. "But they are a decent smoke.

"If you would prefer, I got a box of Gurka Blacks in the car. And I think I have one Maya left."

He handed me a thick cigar, all spotted like it had mould.

"Like I said, Gord. Got a Maya or a Gurka. Like one of

those?"

I was not thinking of the spots on the cigar. I was considering the price. King of Denmark sells for $4,500 for a single cigar.

A box of Gurka Black will set you back twenty grand. Maya cigars are a legend; or almost.

So I took that King and made like I knew all about them and he handed me a silver cigar nipper. We fired up together and sat back to watch the clouds.

"Think I always liked a good smoke," said Barry Water as he took a big puff.

I took just a taste as I told him of my first 'gar'.

He agreed that strong tobacco can do that and explained about some different strains, then said.

"Gord, Water is a good name and an old one but for me, it was a bit of a nuisance. Not the Water name as such, but my first names; Bartholomew Holden Water. Barry for short.

"When I was a lad, the other boys would tease me saying. 'Ha, ha. There goes Barely Holding Water', and I was skinny and couldn't fight too well so I took it."

"Some of the girls would joke, 'Don't go out with him. Barry can't hold his water,' . . . that kind of stuff."

"I always figured I'd show them who's who. Barry holds his water pretty good these days."

Barry took a swig of his beer. "Not in a hurry, Gord? Nice afternoon to sit and talk."

I was not in a hurry and that King was starting to taste good. Barry continued.

"I was not very lucky back in those days, Gord. I wanted to be an explorer or something then, but I had no money for that.

"My first job was in a legal office, writing up contracts.

I liked that and had a good feel for a pen. That all ended when the lawyer absconded with the trust fund.

I found out about a man who had a farm for sale cheap. That's how I got here."

Barry took a puff.

"Turned out the soil was mostly sand and worn out by the time I arrived but all my savings were in this place and I had no choice.

"This house was not here then though. The only house on the place was that old cabin I mentioned before, just over there. Grown up in trees now."

Even after half a beer and three hits on that cigar, I still could not make sense out of the timeline. He was talking about having moved in here four years past, let alone that a cabin could be overgrown in that time period. 2012 to 2015?

I told Barry I was a little confused on exactly when he had lived here. He said he left in '12.

"1912, Gord. Not 2012. I pulled out to see the world 104 years ago this day. Never looked back."

I took a double look at the cigar Barry H. Water had given me. Thinking to stub it out, try this later on when I was alone.

But Barry said, "Like I said, Gord. It's a bit of a tale."

So we decided that the Kings were a good smoke and Barry Water went on.

"Seemed back then I was always on the wrong side of the fight."

I asked him which fight he was speaking of and Barry said the fight between the Devil and the Lord.

I took a second double look at the cigar as Barry continued.

"It was a different time and a different place back in the

new century . . . 1900's, Gord. I mean people did not live in towns so much then and there were folk all round these hills.

"Nice farms in Avoca, and up on the Harrington line. Pointe-au-Chene was getting a new asbestos mine. Calumet was booming with the sawmill and the new power company. Grenville had a train station and the Kilmar mine was feeding a refractory at Marelan.

"But as the people came in the great fight began. You see, the Devil would run around building taverns and the Lord would follow building churches. They fought it out all over the country, but here it was rough.

"I wouldn't have known much about all that except the Devil explained it to me one night.

"He told me that when the new big church opened in Hawkesbury on a Sunday morning, hardly any of the local men were there to see. Seems the devil had a new place opening the night before in Grenville and half of Hawkesbury had not got home till four a.m.

"Guess the Lord got real mad at the devil that day and appeared in a blaze of light right over the devil's tavern. Of course there was nobody there to see cause it was the middle of the afternoon and the place did not open until it was dark enough you could see the red light.

"But the Lord didn't know that so when he appeared in a great flash, it didn't quite come out as planned. The Lord thundered out, 'Devil, keep your pigpens shut'!

"The Devil ignored him and just kept sweeping the sawdust off the floor; getting ready for opening happy hour. Eventually after a bunch of flashes, the Lord had to give it up because he was running out of energy and no one was paying any never mind.

"Before he took off for heaven, the Lord gave a last

attempt and knocked on the tavern door. When the devil opened it to toss the sawdust, the Lord thundered, 'Devil! Keep your pigpens closed'!

"Devil just threw the old sawdust on the street and said to the lord, 'Keep your pigs at home. They mess up my floors'.

'Want one for the road, Lord'? Devil asked, and when the Lord shook his head, the devil went back to work.

"Of course the Lord won some rounds, too, like when he started the temperance society to fight the Devil's drink and the Devil's dance, and got the women to try and keep the men at home.

"Didn't bother the Devil too much. He opened a new tavern in Pointe-au-Chene; right by the mine entry. Then built Harry's Whorehouse up along the Rouge the next fall.

"The devil told me some stories. Not a bad guy once you get to know him.

"Still got time, Gord? These cigars last pretty well and I have a bit of my favourite 'whiskey blanc' in the car. Kind of fun now, remembering those days.

"I have not seen the Devil in a while. Miss those conversations."

I had mostly forgotten about what started this story but it sounded interesting. My King was still about half; Barry's was three quarters gone.

"The neighbours up here were all part of the great fight, Gord. Even your granddad Arthur."

I asked how.

"Well, when the crops were good, they praised the Lord. When things went bad, they cursed the Devil and they went round and round.

"The Lord would preach that a life full of troubles here was a small price to pay for eternity in heaven.

"The Devil, he was always trying to promote dancing and drinking; and Harry's Whorehouse for he had a lot of time invested in that project."

Barry Water smiled at old memories and asked if my cigar was good. It was and getting better.

"Nice afternoon to sit and reminisce," he said and I agreed.

"I moved up here to the old cabin in 1890 with a horse, and a wagon, some farming tools and buckwheat seed. Worked like a madman.

"Got a good crop too. A whole wagon load of sacks, full of buckwheat.

"I took that wagon-load of buckwheat down to Calumet, but on the way, a wheel broke. So I rode the horse to Calumet to get the wheel fixed. When I got back, my wagon was missing so there I was with a wheel and no wagon.

"Next year, I decided to try corn, figuring to sell that by the cob. It grew well here, except the weeds grew well too and I was constantly picking.

"Just when those cobs were all ripe and juicy, the raccoons showed up and ate almost every kernel.

"The man who was to buy my corn saw that and said he had just the solution for my troubles. A 'coon hound' he called it. Big hairy beast.

"This man said that coon hounds could catch a coon faster than spit. He didn't tell me how much coon hounds ate.

"So I fed that coon hound, Fang, and next spring I planted another batch of corn over in that field."

Barry Water pointed a tanned finger at where a young forest was growing. "Yep. Right there was my cornfield. Still got time, Gord?"

I like stories and sometimes even take notes. Not today, though. Too much trouble.

Our beers were near done but I had no more. Barry asked if I was using the old well for water and I said yes.

"Wouldn't mind a bit of that if it's not too much trouble, Gord. It's good water."

So I went off to get some and when I returned with a pitcher and two glasses, Barry was coming back up the steps with a silver flask in his hand.

I poured us out each a glass and set them on the table between. Barry opened up the flask and said.

"Tastes even better with a touch of this, Gord. My special. Made my first batch in the old cabin. Got it much better now. Like a touch in your water, Gord?'

So he poured about one finger's worth in our glasses.

"Got to remember to always put this stuff in water, not the other way around. Dangerous. And don't smoke if you're drinking it straight.

"Take a taste, Gord."

I sipped very lightly, then a little more but there was no flavour. Just like plain water, so I said such to Barry Water.

"Even right out of the flask it has no taste, Gord. Just a hair under two hundred proof. A special blend, Water's water, I call it.

So we settled back for some Water's water and he carried on about coon hounds.

"That Fang dog just about ate me out of house and home by the next fall. But I was ready for them racoons when they showed up.

"Heard them crunching and munching and Fang had his hair all up and growling. So I waited until it seemed there must be the whole gang of coons in my corn field and then I sikked Fang on them.

"Fang, he took off into the cornfield and I never saw him again. Heard a man over in Rawcliff had one just like him later on.

"Anyway, the coons finished off my corn and that's when I started cursing the Devil.

"I got me a pipe and some tobacco and some whiskey blanc, and I sat at my table and cursed him up and down. I had a couple of choice words for the Lord that night too.

"In the middle of a blue streak of curses, there in my kitchen appeared the Devil. Kind of red coloured, with little horns and a weird smile. Had a tail sticking out from under his jacket.

"Didn't see where he came from, but there he was and he says to me. 'Don't get so worked up Barry. I'm just doing my job. If you want to get mad at somebody, blame the Lord. He is always holding the good stuff off till tomorrow. Not like me'.

"Just then a little shiny butterfly or something landed on my shoulder. 'Can't trust that guy', the little voice says. 'He always has some trick up his sleeve'.

"The Devil did have some big sleeves on his coat, but he kind of kept his arms folded behind his back. 'Barry', the Devil said'. Make you a deal'.

"The little voice said, 'Don't listen to him, Barry'. But the devil just smiled and went on.

"'Here's the deal, Barry. You get the good times now and the grief later. What do you think? Nice things and good booze. Deal for you Barry. Have to give me an answer quick cause Harry is next in line'.

The little shiny butterfly whispered so the Devil would not hear. 'Forget the nice things of earth, Barry, just a few tough years and then it's paradise straight through'.

"I asked the Devil how much time I got for paradise

here and hell later. 'Twenty years', said the Devil. 'No holds barred'.

"So I asked the butterfly how his deal went and he said it could not tell me without looking at the book, and that was somewhere else. 'Have to get back to you on that one. But not to worry, paradise was guaranteed'.

"Put that in writing? I asked that little angel and he said no.

"I asked the same question to the Devil and the Devil said no problem, and whipped out a piece of parchment and a pen.

"I took some business courses back in school Gord. One of the lessons was it is better to have 10 per cent of something than 100 per cent of nothing. And here I was, with the smiling Devil on one side and a cute little angel on the other.

"One would put it in writing here and now; the other had to go back to the office and get some details. Didn't seem much a question which was better, so I told the butterfly his terms were poor and he needed a better sales pitch, then sat down at the table to make a deal.

"The Devil started to write but his hand was a little shaky, so he says, 'Want to do the writing, Barry'? and I did and I wrote. 'The Devil, being the party of the first part. And Bartholomew Holden Water being the party of the second part do hereby agree...

"The Devil was getting itchy while I wrote in all the fine print. He had a couple of freebee souls waiting up in Harrington if he could make it by midnight.

"So we signed, the Devil and me with the butterfly as witness, on the front and initialled the back: Twenty years of uninterrupted happiness after which the Devil would have me to fill one of his vacancies in hell. How could I lose?

"The Devil gave me an evil kind of grin and I grinned back just before he disappeared into an old stump. Which is where he must have come from in the first place. The shiny little angel just kind of fluttered off."

Barry asked me how I liked Water's water and I said it tasted just like water. He offered some more. This time he just tossed a splash in my glass. Barry did the same with his, then we watched a cloud.

"They used to grow tobacco up here in those days, Gord. Not much for quality like this." Barry said.

"After the Devil left, I was still wondering how the deal would go down. Tobacco seemed like a start because you can plant 40 acres of the stuff on two thimbles of seed. No need for a wagon.

Hard to start, though, so I went to a farm near St. Jerome where Mr. Quesnel was growing some high grade.

"The farmers up here would start early in the year with those tiny seeds and do all kinds of things before planting. Me, I just went out to my field on a breezy day and tossed those seeds to the wind and lo and behold, rows came up straight as arrows.

"Life got real easy and for a while I kind of went overboard with a new drying shed, this house, and a fancy new wagon with two spare wheels. Since I like the whiskey blanc, I got me the finest of distillers – cost a fortune.

"Devil showed up one night, complaining of the bills and all the trouble it took to get that tobacco seed going and into straight lines.

"I took out the contract and showed him section C, sub-section 4, paragraph 8, line 17, which clearly stated that all bills were to be sent to hell.

"Devil said he thought he was starting to need glasses and looked a little closer at the fine print. Sure enough, there it was and he headed off to study up on distilling.

"I am not a greedy man, Gord. All I ever really wanted was a good smoke and fine whiskey and get around a bit. Do some exploring.

"The Devil sent somebody to pick my crop for me and paid me double the price. As was outlined in the contract in paragraph L, section 11, subsection 18, line 32.

I spent a lot of my time working on tobacco strains and making good whiskey. Keeping one step ahead of the Devil. Went to Cuba and Africa. Even went to see how the Mayans had done it.

"While I was with the Mayans, I studied up a bit on a drink they make out of a cactus; not much for alcohol but what a kick. I brought some of that joy juice back here with me.

"When my birthday came around that year I looked in the mirror and noticed a little gray. I immediately reminded the Devil of paragraph D, section 2, sub-section 18, line 13, which clearly stated that I was not to age during the life of this contract.

"Devil had brought a set of reading glasses when he came because he said he did not think that was included. After looking at that small print with glasses, he seemed to turn a little pink; like he was reading it for the first time. He quit before he got done the second page.

"I let him off easy because a little grey looks good. But I reminded him of the paragraph which had to do with wrinkles.

"Headed right back down that tree stump with not so much as a fare thee well.

"I did not see him much after that except when he showed up to complain about my travel expenses. I took the contract out and was about to show him paragraph M when he said never mind.

"Devil started going on about how the print was too fine and I told him he should have brought a bigger parchment then he asked me if I knew how much good parchment cost these days.

"He went back down that stump hole complaining about the cost of heat in hell and how he was having a hard time getting the respect he deserved."

Barry and me, we watched a cloud go by and by now he was finished his King and mine was just lying in the ashtray on the table.

"How's your water doing, Gord? Like a drop more?"

I said I was doing fine but Barry he asked to be excused for a moment and went down the steps to his Beamer. He came back with a tobacco pouch and two old-fashioned pipes. Like you see in a museum, made of clay with curved stems.

Barry Water opened up the pouch and pulled out some cut-up tobacco, a dark pink colour.

"My own special strain of tobacco, Gord. Made this one up myself while waiting for the contract to come to terms."

Barry stuffed the two pipes and set one in the ashtray.

"I'll leave that pipe with you, Gord. Try it out sometime but be careful. It is a tad strong. Sweet but strong."

Barry fired up on his pipe and a contented look came over him. Like what a cat looks like after it ate a mouse.

"You know how time flies, Gord. Them 20 years just kind of flew by. Life was easy for me. Couldn't make a mistake if I tried; and I did try.

"Almost blew this place up finding out what happens when you double distil.

"Travelled a lot then, too, exploring and checking out the beaches, that type of thing. To keep the Devil from complaining too much, I skipped the five-star places and travelled first-class instead of private.

"I brought tobacco seed back from where ever I found good smoke and blended all those strains to make what I have in this pouch. Rose de Quesnel, I call it.

"Like I said, Gord. It is powerful smoke." We both glanced down at that pipe in the ashtray looking like some museum piece.

"No more smoke for me today, Barry," I told him. "Tastes real smooth but I have a few bad memories of tobacco."

"The Devil has a few himself now, Gord." Barry took another pull on his pipe and went back to memory lane.

"Twenty years to the minute the Devil came out of that stump. But now he had to walk farther because I was living here and not in the old cabin.

"He came right into the kitchen and told me his troubles were finished but mine were about to begin and said to pack a toothbrush.

"I told the Devil I'd get my toothbrush in a minute but in the meantime he could review Section Y, sub-section 17, paragraph 6, line 33 which clearly stated that we were to share one drink and one pipe at the mentioned kitchen table before we headed off.

"I laid out two pipes, just like these Gord, and I poured two shot glasses of my special Water's water. Triple-distilled with some of that Mayan joy juice for flavour. It adds a certain 'je ne sais quoi' to the brew.

"So I sat at one side of the table and the Devil sat on the other. He was real happy that the payments for my contract were almost finished and he chugged that Water's water back as if it was tequila.

"This was Devil's night to party so I asked him if he would like a second to wash down the first. He dropped that quicker than the first and I let the vapours go away before we lit the pipes.

"One for the Gipper, I told the Devil, but he did not know who the Gipper was. I volunteered to tell him but he said no. Only a couple of puffs and we were off to his place, he said.

"So the Devil, he took one long draw on my Rose de Quesnel, inhaled it too, and the strangest thing happened. Guess that Mayan joy juice was kicking in; his eyes crossed, then the Devil's pupils got real big.

"Then the Devil started to turn a weird shade of orange. Poor old guy just headed straight back to his hollow stump. Never bothered to sign off on the non-completion part; section A, sub-section 3, paragraph 6, which said that if the conditions of Section Y, sub-section 9, were not completed . . .

"When Devil showed up the next night looking like one of those Kermit the Frog dolls kids play with these days and wanted me to go with him, I reminded him of the aforementioned sections and paragraphs and he said he'd have to come back to go over that.

"Devil came back a two nights later looking a little better and telling me of all the strange things that happened in hell after he left my house; wanting to have a good look at that contract he had signed. He brought three-power reading glasses this time.

"He sat at my kitchen table and read for about an hour and a half and grumbled about my small handwriting.

"After reading and checking one side against the other, Devil said to me. 'Straight up, Barry. How much will it cost me to get out of this deal?'

"I told him I could write us up a contract. The Devil was a little leery of that idea and preferred we work something out on a handshake. I reminded him that contracts were his idea in the first place.

"We sat and he told of how things were not so good for him as they had been 20 years ago. The spot market for souls was down to a dime a dozen, and the futures were heading south.

"I reminded him of the section which dealt with financial responsibilities of the party of the first part and the Devil groaned.

" 'Damn details, he said', and I agreed, but contracts are contracts. So we worked out a payment schedule for the old guy and set only main parts of the original contract.

"I let the Devil off easy since the default section meant he would have had to pay me double. I wrote just a few words on a large piece of parchment. The Devil didn't want any small print.

"I get medical, dental; travel expenses paid and all the smoke I want. Make my own whiskey blanc so the bar bill is pretty small.

"Well, Gord. Best be on my way. Got a thing or two to do before me and the Devil meet tonight over at the old hollow stump. He's coming to give me a forward on the next five years expenses, estimated, of course, with inflation running high and the Canadian dollar down . . .

"Got to run," Barry Water said as he put on his panama. "Got to go get ready for the Devil. He won't touch my Rose, but he like a good cigar now and then.

Barry stood up and stretched. The sun was getting low and there were still no clouds to watch. Before Barry started down my steps he said.

"I always like to have something special when we meet. The Devil got peeved at me when he found out about the Mayan joy juice in his whiskey. Went on about informed consent and I told him that was not in our contract. So he brings his own bottle now.

"While I was in Santa Marta this spring, enjoying their mountains, I had the boys roll me up some of their smokables inside good tobacco leaf.

"Curious to find out how the old guy likes the mix. Course I don't intend to tell him unless he asks. We agreed no more Maya joy juice but didn't say anything about cigars.

"Got a couple rolled up in the car, Gord. Like one?"

I said no, thanks, because Jerome down the road grows some stuff that will make an elephant fly.

Barry asked if I would introduce him to Jerome, next time around. Maybe trade with Jerome for some good cigars.

I told Barry Water that Jerome would probably go for that deal.

Barry said that would give us an opportunity to sit and have a beer, or some Water's water. He could give me an update on how the Columbian went over with the Devil.

Bartholomew Holden Water was just about to get in his seven series when he stopped, grabbed something under the seat and came back up the steps lively as a butterfly.

He handed me a little pouch of his Rose de Quesnel and a silver flask, then said, "This here is my private smoke, Gord. One puff equals two of these here cigars. And a flask of my finest triple-distilled Water's water. Complete with Maya joy juice.

"In case the Devil shows up. He doesn't even want to

see that stuff. Makes him turn orange just to look."

Barry turned his Beamer around and as he was driving out, he rolled down the window.

"By the way, Gord. If you see some strange happenings over at the old cabin tonight it is probably just the Devil. That Columbian seems to make time go real slow.

"Next meeting maybe, I can show you a video or two of the old guy in slow-mo. I keep one of them cell phones with me and a picture is worth a thousand words, they say.

"Devil's reputation might fall apart if pictures hit Twitter of him trying to figure a way down a hollow stump.

"Nothing in our contract that says no pictures.

"Got to run, Gord. Meet you again."

Nice guy, that Barry Water. But never make a contract with him. Even the Devil got lost in the fine print.

Acknowledgements

Special thanks to Louise Sproule for her encouragement and enthusiasm, and to Jill Crosby for her excellent art. I extend thanks to my neighbour, photographer Mads Modeweg, for the image on the cover of this book.